GREATER MANCHESTER'S PUBLIC SWIMMING POOLS

ROCHDALE

OLDHAM

WIGAN

MANCHESTER

TAMESIDE

STOCKPORT

A PICTORIAL GUIDE BY J.C. MATHER

Published by Rossendale Books

11 MowgrainView, Bacup,

Rossendale, Lancashire

OL13 8EJ

England

Published in paperback 2012

Copyright © John C. Mather 2012

ISBN: 978-1-291-11790-5

Dedication

Dedicated to my late parents, John and Margaret;

with special thanks to my brother, Robert.

Acknowledgements

Thanks to Beth and Louise for their continuing support,

and to Harry for all his invaluable assistance.

CONTENTS

FOREWORD BY J.C.MATHER

I HOPE THIS GUIDE GOES SOME WAY TO CELEBRATING SWIMMING IN GREATER MANCHESTER.

AFTER ALL, THERE IS A WEALTH OF PUBLIC SWIMMING POOLS IN THE REGION - AND A GRAND TRADITION OF LEISURE SWIMMING AND OLYMPIC SUCCESS.

THOUGH, ITS SAD TO HEAR OF POOLS HAVING TO CLOSE BECAUSE OF FINANCIAL CUTS...

OF COURSE GREATER MANCHESTER CONTAINS A FASCINATING + DIVERSE COLLECTION OF TOWNS AND PEOPLE - AND I HAVE TRIED TO INCLUDE SOMETHING MEMORABLE OR SPECIAL ABOUT EACH POOL'S LOCATION.

FINALLY, I EXTEND A BIG "THANK YOU" TO EVERYONE WHO HAS HELPED AND ENCOURAGED ME TO COMPILE THIS GUIDE.

HAPPY SWIMMING!

J.C.Mather, 2012

SUMMARY OF GREATER MANCHESTER'S POOLS

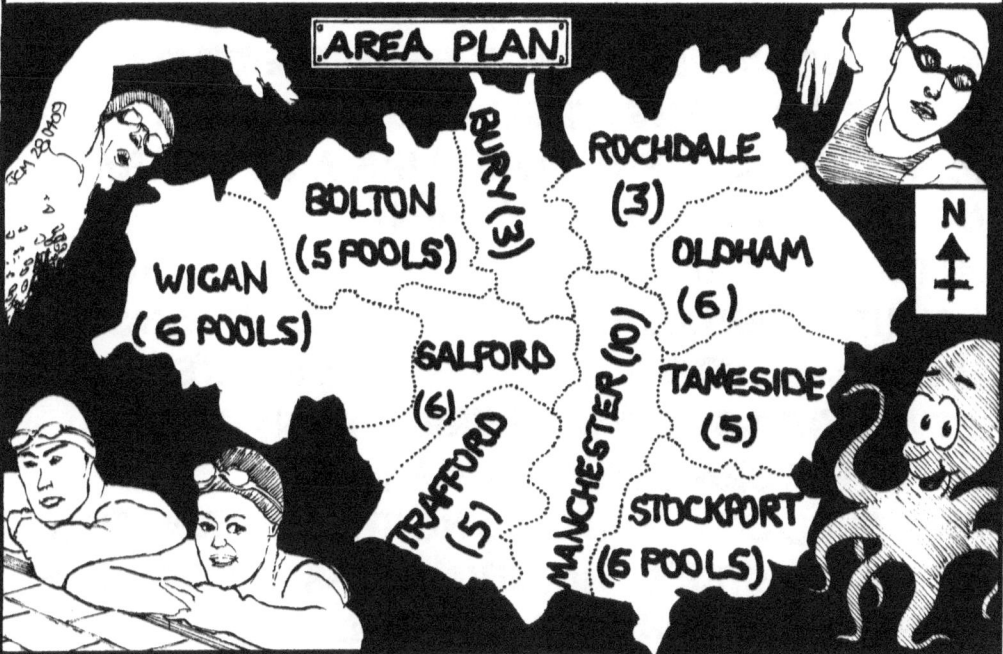

AREA PLAN

ROCHDALE (3)

BOLTON (5 POOLS)

BURY (3)

OLDHAM (6)

WIGAN (6 POOLS)

SALFORD (6)

MANCHESTER (10)

TAMESIDE (5)

TRAFFORD (5)

STOCKPORT (6 POOLS)

N

THIS GUIDE COVERS ALL 55 PUBLIC POOLS WITHIN GREATER MANCHESTER'S 10 COUNCILS; AND LISTS THEM IN THE FOLLOWING, CLOCKWISE SEQUENCE:-

- MANCHESTER CITY COUNCIL
- TRAFFORD METROPOLITAN BOROUGH COUNCIL
- SALFORD CITY COUNCIL
- WIGAN METROPOLITAN BOROUGH COUNCIL
- BOLTON METROPOLITAN BOROUGH COUNCIL
- BURY METROPOLITAN BOROUGH COUNCIL
- ROCHDALE METROPOLITAN BOROUGH COUNCIL
- OLDHAM METROPOLITAN BOROUGH COUNCIL
- TAMESIDE METROPOLITAN BOROUGH COUNCIL
- STOCKPORT METROPOLITAN BOROUGH COUNCIL

INTRODUCTION

I LEARNT TO SWIM IN BURY'S SPECTACULAR VICTORIAN BATHS. IT SEEMED NOT JUST A PLACE TO SWIM BUT MORE LIKE A LANDMARK OF CIVIC PRIDE AND OPULENCE.

ALTHOUGH IT WAS REPLACED BY A MODERN LEISURE CENTRE IN THE 1970'S I ALWAYS HARBOURED GREAT AFFECTION FOR BURY'S OLD STYLE BATHS AND WONDERED IF ANY OTHER ARCHITECTURAL GEMS REMAINED.

THE PUBLICITY SURROUNDING THE RESTORATION OF MANCHESTER'S VICTORIA BATHS INSPIRED ME TO FIND OUT FOR MYSELF. AND SO I SET MYSELF A CHALLENGE - TO SWIM IN EVERY PUBLIC SWIMMING POOL IN GREATER MANCHESTER. YOU COULD CALL MY RESULTING GUIDE "A LABOUR OF LOVE" BECAUSE THE TASK PROVED MUCH LARGER THAN I HAD FIRST IMAGINED. AFTER ALL, THERE ARE OVER 50 PUBLIC POOLS WITHIN THE REGION'S TEN METROPOLITAN BOROUGHS!

MY GUIDE IS NOT INTENDED TO COMPARE OR JUDGE POOLS - I TREAT EACH POOL ON ITS OWN MERITS, BE IT AN ART DÉCOR MASTERPIECE OR A PLAIN OLD UTILITARIAN CONCRETE AND GLASS "SHELL." I ONLY HOPE THAT IT HELPS RECOGNISE THESE ASSETS FOR THEIR TRUE WORTH -

INTRODUCTION

THE OUTCRY ARISING FROM PROPOSALS TO CLOSE LEVENSHULME POOL IN 2011 ONLY SERVES TO PROVE SWIMMING'S UNIQUE AND OFTEN UNDERSTATED ROLE IN SOCIETY.

PART OF THE ENJOYMENT OF VISITING EACH POOL WAS NEVER QUITE KNOWING WHAT I WOULD FIND. TAKE THE CITY OF MANCHESTER'S LARGE STOCK OF POOLS, FOR EXAMPLE, WHICH CONTAINS A BEWILDERING ARRAY OF ARCHITECTURAL STYLES AND FACILITIES!

IT IS PLEASING TO KNOW THAT SEVERAL OLD STYLE BATHS STILL REMAIN - PRIDE OF PLACE MUST GO TO OLDHAM MBC'S COMPTON POOL WHICH DATES FROM 1899 AND IS THE OLDEST IN THE REGION.

MY VISITS HAVE ALSO GIVEN ME AN INSIGHT INTO A LONG FORGOTTEN "GOLDEN AGE" OF SWIMMING PRIOR TO THE FIRST WORLD WAR. GREATER MANCHESTER'S SWIMMERS LITERALLY LED THE WORLD AND CHADDERTON'S HENRY TAYLOR WON THREE GOLD MEDALS AT THE 1908 LONDON OLYMPICS.

IT HAS BEEN A PLEASURE TO VISIT SO MANY THRIVING POOLS AND ENJOY SWIMMING'S CONTINUING POPULARITY.

HOW THIS GUIDE WORKS

CONTACT DETAILS

ADDRESS: HILL COT RO

PHONE/FAX: 0120 433

WEB/E-MAIL: SHARPLES.

OWNER: BOLTON ME

WHY DON'T YOU CHECK POOL TIMES BEFORE SETTING OUT?

EXPLAINING THOSE PLANS — SEE EXAMPLE, BELOW:

MAIN ROAD	▬▬▬	FREE PARKING		P
SIDE ROAD/STREET	═══	PAY PARKING		PP
ACCESS TO POOL	••••••	DISABLED PARKING		⊖P
FOOTPATH	•••••••			

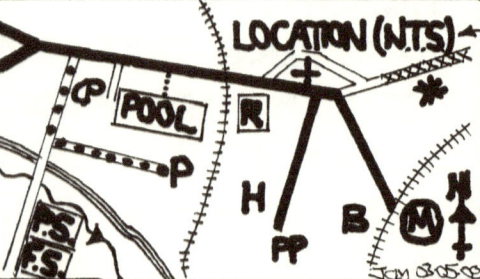

LOCATION (N.T.S) — NOT TO SCALE!

CANAL

RIVER

PLACE OF WORSHIP		+
SHOPPING AREA		✱
PRECINCT		∞∞∞

POLICE STATION	P.S.	RAILWAY/METRO		┼┼┼┼┼
FIRE STATION	F.S.	RAILWAY STATION		R
HOSPITAL	H	METRO STATION		Ⓜ
		BUS/COACH STATION		B

IT'S DEAD SIMPLE..

N.B. ALL VIEWS EXPRESSED IN THIS GUIDE ARE THOSE OF J.C. MATHER AND MAY NOT REFLECT THE VIEWS OF THE RELEVANT LOCAL AUTHORITIES

ABRAHAM MOSS LEISURE CENTRE

ADDRESS: CRESCENT RD., CRUMPSALL, MCR., M8 5UF
PHONE/FAX: 0161 720 7622/0161 720 9329
WEB/E-MAIL: info.abrahammoss@leisure.serco.com
OWNER: MANCHESTER CITY COUNCIL

ABRAHAM MOSS COMPLEX   JEWISH MUSEUM

THIS SUPERB CENTRE IS AN IMPORTANT RESOURCE
FOR THE LOCAL AND DIVERSE COMMUNITIES OF
CRUMPSALL + CHEETHAM IN NORTH MANCHESTER.
OPENED IN 1973 AND REFURBISHED IN 2000/2,
IT OFFERS • SWIMMING POOL 25M × 5 LANES
          • FITNESS STUDIO/WORK OUT STUDIO
          • HEALTH SUITE AND SMALL POOL
          • PARKING ON SITE (FREE)

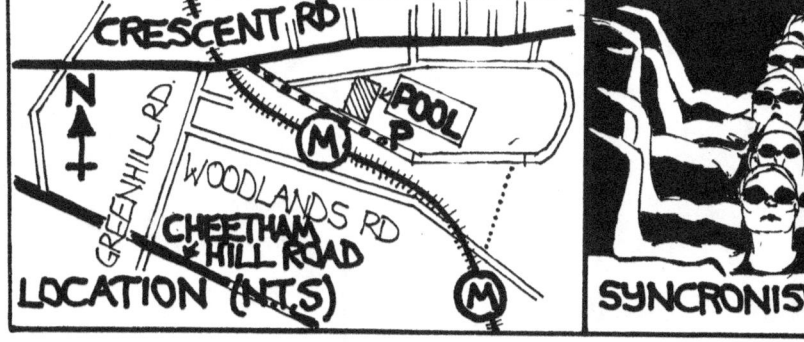

LOCATION (N.T.S)   SYNCRONISED TAI CHI?

BROADWAY LEISURE CENTRE

ADDRESS: BROADWAY, NEW MOSTON, M/C, M40 3LN
PHONE/FAX: 0161 681 1060/
WEB/E-MAIL: info.broadway@leisure.serco.com
OWNER: MANCHESTER CITY COUNCIL

ELEVATION

ATISHOO!
BANISH THE WINTER FLUS AND START SWIMMING

BUILT IN 1932 "TO IMPROVE THE HEALTH AND WELL BEING OF THE LOCAL COMMUNITY", THE OLD BROADWAY BATHS HAVE BEEN RENNOVATED TO CREATE A FIRST CLASS LEISURE CENTRE OFFERING:

- POOL 25M × 4 LANES
- FITNESS/HEALTH SUITE

LOCAL RESIDENT, SAM QUINN, HAS SWUM AT THIS POOL FOR OVER 75 YEARS!

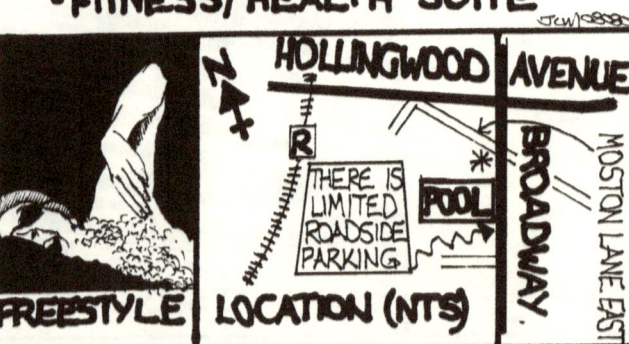

FREESTYLE

HOLLINGWOOD AVENUE

R

THERE IS LIMITED ROADSIDE PARKING

POOL

BROADWAY

MOSTON LANE EAST

LOCATION (NTS)

IS THIS A RECORD?

CHORLTON LEISURE CENTRE

ADDRESS: MANCHESTER ROAD, CHORLTON-CUM-HARDY
MANCHESTER, M21 9PQ

PHONE/FAX: 0161 8610790/

WEB/E-MAIL: info.chorlton@leisure.serco.com

OWNER: MANCHESTER CITY COUNCIL

ELEVATION

HENRY PRICE,
MANCHESTER
CITY ARCHITECT
+ POOL LEGEND.

OPENED ON 19 SEPTEMBER 1929, THIS CHARMING
AND OLD FASHIONED POOL IS A POPULAR FEATURE
OF THIS COSMOPOLITAN SUBURB. IT RETAINS
MANY ORIGINAL ITEMS, LIKE POOLSIDE CUBICLES
AND THE STONE STEPS! WHY NOT SEE FOR YOURSELF?
IT OFFERS: • SWIMMING POOL 22.4M × 7.5M (73'6")
• SAUNA / FITNESS STUDIO GYM
• FREE CAR PARKING.

WILBRAHAM ROAD
LIBRARY
MANCHESTER ROAD
KENSINGTON ROAD
POOL P
→ Z
LOCATION (NTS)
JCM 240B10

EASY PEASY!

STARTING 'EM YOUNG!

FORUM LEISURE CENTRE

ADDRESS: FORUM SQUARE, WYTHENSHAWE, MANCHESTER, M22 5RX

PHONE/FAX: 0161 935 4020 / 0161 935 4016

WEB/E-MAIL: info.forum@leisure.serco.com

OWNER: MANCHESTER CITY COUNCIL

ENTRANCE TO FORUM

DANCER AT THE FORUM'S ONE WORLD EVENT

OPENED IN 1971, THE REFURBISHED FORUM PROVIDES "A VIBRANT MODERN CENTRE" TO THIS CHALLENGING AREA. FACILITIES ARE SUPERB + OFFER:

- MAIN POOL - 25M × 6 LANES
- TRAINING POOL
- FITNESS STUDIO + HEALTH SUITE
- CAR PARKING ON SITE (FREE)

LOCATION (NTS)

KEEP FIT: ENJOY LIFE

SWIMMING IS FOR EVERY BODY!

LEVENSHULME SWIMMING POOLS

ADDRESS: BARLOW ROAD, LEVENSHULME, MANCHESTER, M19 3HE
PHONE/FAX: 0161 224 4370 / 0161 225 8378
WEB/E-MAIL: info.levenshulmepool @ leisure.serco.com
OWNER: MANCHESTER CITY COUNCIL

THE BATHS

LORD FOSTER, ARCHITECT, WAS BORN HERE IN 1935

BERLIN'S REICHSTAG

THE MULTI-CULTURAL SUBURB OF LEVENSHULME IS A POPULAR HOME FOR PEOPLES OF IRISH AND PAKISTANI DESCENT. OPENED IN 1931, "THE BATHS" COST £23,950 TO BUILD! MANY OF THE ORIGINAL, INTRICATE FEATURES ADORN THE:

- MAIN POOL 22·9m × 7·6m
- LEARNER POOL 18·3m × 6·1m
- GYM PLUS SAUNA + STEAM ROOM

WHY NOT ENJOY A RELAXING MASSAGE!

R

ROADSIDE PARKING IS VERY LIMITED!

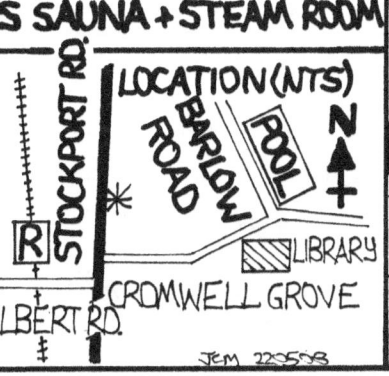

LOCATION (NTS)

STOCKPORT RD.
BARLOW ROAD
POOL
N
R
ALBERT RD.
CROMWELL GROVE
LIBRARY

JEM 220508

MANCHESTER AQUATICS CENTRE

ADDRESS: 2 BOOTH STREET EAST, OXFORD ROAD,
ARDWICK, MANCHESTER, M13 9SS
PHONE/FAX: 0161 275 9450/
WEB/E-MAIL: info.manchesteraquatics@leisure.serco.com
OWNER: MANCHESTER CITY COUNCIL

OXFORD ROAD ELEVATION

MANCHESTER'S STUNNING "AQUATICS CENTRE"
SUCCESFULLY HOSTED THE 2002 COMMONWEALTH
GAMES. DESCRIBED AS "EUROPE'S BIGGEST LEISURE
POOL COMPLEX", THIS POPULAR, CITY CENTRE
LANDMARK WAS BUILT AT A COST OF £32 MILLION
AND OPENED ON 12 OCTOBER 2000 BY
HER MAJESTY QUEEN ELIZABETH THE SECOND.
IT FEATURES: MAIN POOL 50M × 8 LANES
    • TRAINING POOL 50M × 4 LANES
    • LAGOON
    • DIVING POOL
    • FITNESS SUITE/WORK OUT STUDIO
    • HEALTH SUITE

MANCHESTER AQUATICS CENTRE

ENGLAND'S VICTORIOUS WOMEN

THE "MANCHESTER 2002" COMMONWEALTH GAMES ARE SEEN AS A GREAT SUCCESS FOR THE CITY AND POOL, ALIKE. MUCH OF THE INTEREST CENTRED ON AUSTRALIAN SWIMMING CHAMPION IAN "THE THORPEDO" THORPE.

STILL ONLY 19 YEARS OF AGE, HE WON 6 GOLD MEDALS HERE WITH SOME STYLE. MANY REGARD IT AS A PRIVILEGE TO HAVE SEEN "THE WORLD'S GREATEST SWIMMER" IN ACTION!

"THE THORPEDO"

JCM 01.10.10

RECLAIM YOUR PARKING TICKET AT THE POOL

LOCATION (N.T.S.)

DIVING IS NOT ALLOWED!

MILES PLATTING SWIMMING POOLS

ADDRESS: VARLEY ST., MILES PLATTING, M/C , M40 8EE
PHONE/FAX: 0161-205-8939/
WEB/E-MAIL: info.milesplattingpool@leisure.serco.com
OWNER: MANCHESTER CITY COUNCIL

POOL ELEVATION

BOTH THE GREAT BRITAIN AND CITY OF MANCHESTER'S WATER POLO SQUADS TRAIN HERE.

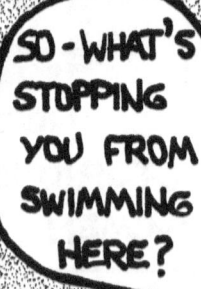

APPEARANCES CAN BE <u>SO</u> DECEPTIVE! OPENED IN 1978, THE POOLS' NO-NONSENSE, INNER CITY FACADE MASKS A REALLY GOOD SWIM. FEATURES INCLUDE:

- MAIN POOL: 25m × 12.5m
- SPECIALIST POOL: 25m × 12.5m
- TRAINING POOL: 9m
- FITNESS GYM
- FREE CAR PARKING

JEM 17·10·10

SO - WHAT'S STOPPING YOU FROM SWIMMING HERE?

NEDUM ONUOHA

ETIHAD

LOCAL FOOTBALLER

LOCATION (NTS)

N

OLDHAM RD.

LIBRARY

POOL P

VARLEY ST.

VICTORIA MILLS

ROCHDALE CANAL

BRADFORD ROAD

MOSS SIDE LEISURE CENTRE

ADDRESS: MOSS LANE EAST, MOSS SIDE, MCR., M15 5NN
PHONE/FAX: 0161 226 5015/6-
WEB/E-MAIL: info.mosssideleisure@leisure.serco.com.
OWNER: MANCHESTER CITY COUNCIL

ELEVATION

HAVE YOU TRIED LANE SWIMMING?

THINGS ARE LOOKING UP FOR MOSS SIDE'S DIVERSE COMMUNITY. AND THE SPACIOUS POOL IS REALLY GOOD! OPENED IN 1970, THIS THRIVING CENTRE OFFERS:

IT ALWAYS SEEMS BUSY IN SCHOOL HOLIDAYS

BREAST-STROKE

- MAIN POOL: 25M x 6 LANES
- TEACHING POOL
- FITNESS + HEALTH SUITES/SAUNA
- SPORTS HALL/WORK OUT STUDIO
- FREE CAR PARKING (U/GROUND)

SWIMMING TAKES ALL MY CARES AWAY-

-I LOVE IT!

HULME HIGH ST.
GREENHEYS LANE
POOL
UNDER GROUND PARKING!
F.S.
PRINCESS ROAD
N
Brewery
MOSS LANE EAST
LOCATION (N.T.S)
© JCM 03-11-10

NORTH CITY FAMILY + FITNESS CENTRE

ADDRESS: UPPER CONRAN ST., HARPURHEY, MCR., M9 4DA
PHONE/FAX: 0161 277 1900/
WEB/E-MAIL: northcityfitness@manchestersportsandleisure.org
OWNER: MANCHESTER CITY COUNCIL

ELEVATION

THE LATE BERNARD MANNING; LOCAL STAR OF STAGE, "EMBASSY CLUB" + POLITICALLY INCORRECT CONTROVERSY

TAKING THE PLUNGE..... (LITERALLY!)

WHAT AN ENJOYABLE POOL! OPENED IN 2005, THIS UNIQUE CENTRE COMBINES SUPERB FACILITIES WITH AN INNOVATIVE "SURE START SCHEME". THE CENTRE OFFERS:

- 25M x 5 LANE POOL WITH MOVABLE FLOOR
- HEALTH SUITE
- EXERCISE STUDIO
- CAR PARKING (FREE)

PLEASE KEEP OUR WATER CLEAN!

OLD HARPURHEY POOL (1911-2001)

ROCHDALE RD

MOSTON LANE

P POOL

UPPER CONRAN ST.

N

LOCATION (N.T.S)

JCM 090909

20

WITHINGTON LEISURE CENTRE

ADDRESS: BURTON RD., WITHINGTON, MANCHESTER, M20 3EB
PHONE/FAX: 0161 445 1046/
WEB/E-MAIL: info.withington@leisure.serco.com
OWNER: MANCHESTER CITY COUNCIL

ELEVATION

MANCHESTER'S FIRST MIXED BATHING WAS TRIALLED HERE IN 1914...

SHOCKING! WHATEVER NEXT?

OPENED IN 1913 AT A COST OF £17,426, THIS SUPERB FACILITY ADDS A CERTAIN CHARM + TRADITION TO THIS LIVELY AND COSMOPOLITAN VILLAGE. THINK "VICTORIA BATHS" ON A SMALLER SCALE AND OFFERING:

MAD FOR IT!

- POOL: 25 YDS × 9 YDS
- FITNESS + WORKOUT STUDIOS
- FREE CAR PARKING

JCM 17·12·10

BILLY MEREDITH

FOOTBALLING SUPERSTAR LIVED HERE

LOCATION (N.T.S.)
WHITCHURCH RD.
POOL
BURTON RD.
PALATINE RD.
WILMSLOW RD.
N

OASIS' NOEL + LIAM GALLAGHER COME FROM NEARBY BURNAGE

ALTRINCHAM LEISURE CENTRE

ADDRESS: OAKFIELD ROAD, ALTRINCHAM, WA15 8EW
PHONE/FAX: 0161 926 3255/
WEB/E-MAIL: WWW.TRAFFORDLEISURE.CO.UK
OWNER: TRAFFORD METROPOLITAN BOROUGH COUNCIL

ELEVATION OF POOL

TIMPERLEY'S LATE GREAT

FRANK SIDEBOTTOM

THIS PROSPEROUS TOWN BOASTS HALF TIMBERED HOUSES + FOOT-BALLERS' WAGS! OPENED IN 1975, THE FRIENDLY CENTRE OFFERS:

- MAIN POOL · 25M x 5L
- TEACHING POOL
- SPORTS HALL / GYM
- CRECHE / SAUNA
- FREE CAR PARKING

JCM 16.11.11

USE YOUR POOL- DON'T LOSE IT!

DUNHAM MASSEY

LOCATION (NTS)

STAMFORD NEW RD.
MR
ICE RINK
PP
P POOL
STATION APPROACH
MOSS LANE
OAKFIELD ROAD ←→ N

PARTINGTON SPORTS VILLAGE

ADDRESS: CHAPEL LANE, PARTINGTON, M/C., M31 4ES
PHONE/FAX: 0161-777-4222/
WEB/E-MAIL: WWW.TRAFFORDLEISURE.CO.UK
OWNER: TRAFFORD METROPOLITAN BOROUGH COUNCIL

ELEVATION

SWIMMING'S A FAMILY THING!

- AND ITS FUN!

SITUATED ON THE SOUTHERN BANK OF THE MANCHESTER SHIP CANAL, SEMI-RURAL PARTINGTON FEATURES SOME OF THE BEST SPORTS + FITNESS FACILITIES AROUND. THESE INCLUDE:

- POOL 20M × 4 LANES (OPENED SEPT. 1982)
- FITNESS SUITE
- SPORTS HALL
- OUTDOOR PITCHES (3G)
- GRASS COURTS
- FREE CAR PARKING

JCM 2605:12

N
WARBURTON LANE
CHAPEL LANE
CROSS LANE WEST
P
POOL
LOCATION (N.T.S.)

BOTH THE GB AND JAPANESE OLYMPIC + BRAZILIAN PARALYMPIC FOOTBALL TEAMS TRAINED HERE FOR THE 2012 GAMES!

WARNING

DIVING IS NOT PERMITTED!

SALE LEISURE CENTRE

ADDRESS: BROAD ROAD, SALE, MANCHESTER, M33 2AL
PHONE/FAX: 0161 905 5588 / 0161 905 5589
WEB/E-MAIL: INFO@TRAFFORDLEISURE.CO.UK
OWNER: TRAFFORD METROPOLITAN BOROUGH COUNCIL

ELEVATION

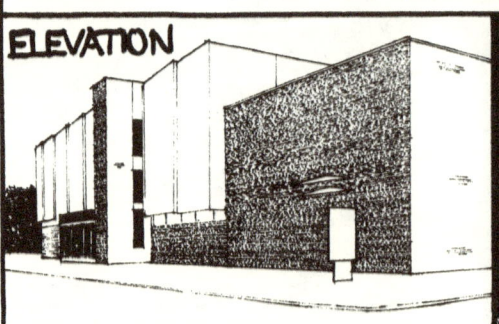

THIS PLEASANT CANAL-SIDE TOWN HOSTS AN IMPRESSIVE CENTRE. OPENED IN 1973, IT OFFERS:

- MAIN POOL: 25M × 6 LANES
- CLUB POOL*: 25 YDS × 10 YDS
- TEACHING POOL
- SPORTS HALL + ZEST GYM
- EXTERNAL CLIMBING WALL
- FREE CAR PARKING

JCM 10·11·11

*THIS USES THE ORIGINAL BATHS FROM THE EARLIER PUBLIC BATHS OPENED IN 1914.

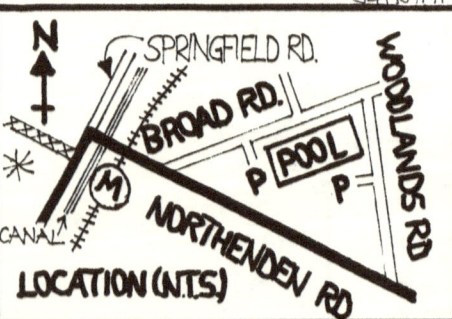

LOCATION (N.T.S.)

STRETFORD LEISURE CENTRE

ADDRESS: GREAT STONE ROAD, STRETFORD, M32 0ZS
PHONE/FAX: 0161-875-1414 / –
WEB/E-MAIL: WWW.TRAFFORD LEISURE.CO.UK
OWNER: TRAFFORD METROPOLITAN BOROUGH COUNCIL

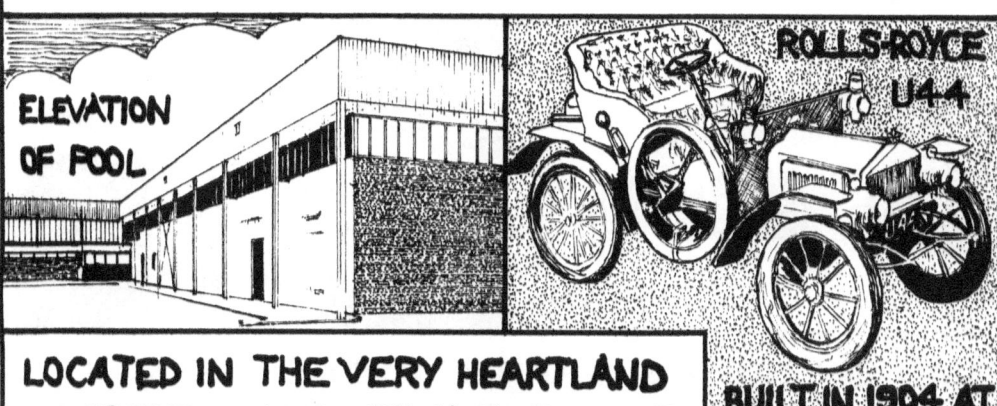

ELEVATION OF POOL

ROLLS-ROYCE U44

LOCATED IN THE VERY HEARTLAND OF SPORTING + INDUSTRIAL EXCELLENCE, THIS CENTRE PROVIDES TOP CLASS FACILITIES. OPENED IN 1977, IT OFFERS:

- MAIN POOL 25m x 6 LANES
- TEACHING POOL
- SPORTS HALL/SQUASH COURT
- GYM / SPINNING STUDIO
- FREE CAR PARKING

BUILT IN 1904 AT TRAFFORD PARK

JCM 29·01·11

JESSICA ENNIS, ATHLETE

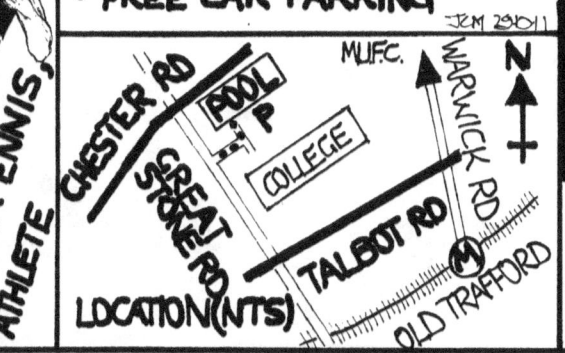

LOCATION (NTS)

CHESTER RD
POOL P
GREAT STONE RD
COLLEGE
M.U.F.C.
WARWICK RD
N
TALBOT RD
OLD TRAFFORD

MAN. UTD.'S CUP WINNING STAR TRIO!

URMSTON LEISURE CENTRE

ADDRESS: BOWFELL RD., FLIXTON, MCR., M41 5RR
PHONE/FAX: 0161-749-2570/
WEB/E-MAIL: INFO @ TRAFFORDLEISURE.CO.UK
OWNER: TRAFFORD METROPOLITAN BOROUGH COUNCIL

ELEVATION

-FIND TIME TO SWIM!

THEY SAY THAT THE CHARMING TOWN OF URMSTON
BEARS THE HEART OF A VILLAGE. OPENED IN 1989,
THIS IMPRESSIVE CENTRE INCLUDES A LIBRARY + POOL
WITH INNOVATIVE HIGH TECH. ADJUSTABLE WATER DEPTH.

IT OFFERS: • MAIN POOL 25M × 5 L
• TEACHING POOL
• FITNESS SUITE/SAUNA
• SPORTS HALL
• FREE CAR PARKING

FACT
THE NHS,
NATIONAL
HEALTH
SERVICE, WAS
FOUNDED AT
TRAFFORD
GENERAL
HOSPITAL
IN 1948

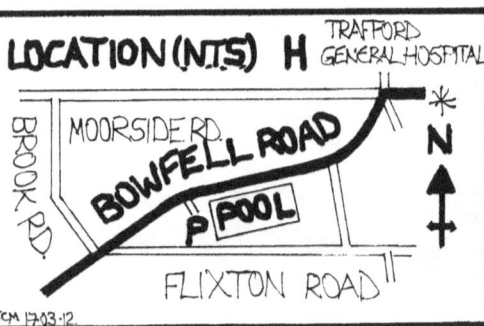

LOCATION (N.T.S)
H TRAFFORD GENERAL HOSPITAL
BROOK RD.
MOORSIDE RD.
BOWFELL ROAD
P POOL
FLIXTON ROAD
N
JCM 17.03.12.

BARTON AQUEDUCT

26

BROUGHTON   POOL

ADDRESS: GREAT CHEETHAM ST., WEST, SALFORD, M7 2DN
PHONE/FAX: 0161 792 2847/
WEB/E-MAIL: fit city broughton pool@scll.co.uk
OWNER: SALFORD CITY COUNCIL

ELEVATION

ELKIE BROOKS, SINGER

"ONE OF THE GREAT UK. VOICES"

JOHN COOPER CLARKE

SALFORD POET

BROUGHTON HAS SO MANY ARTISTIC CONNECTIONS - AND THE POOL'S NOT BAD EITHER! OPENED IN 1967, IT OFFERS THIS DIVERSE AREA.
- MAIN POOL 25M × 6 LANES
- TEACHING POOL
- HEALTH + FITNESS SUITE
- PARKING ON SITE (FREE)

WARNING!

HIC!

DON'T DRINK + DIVE!

GREAT CHEETHAM ST. W.
GREAT CLOWES ST.
PENTLAND AV.
BURY NEW RD.
P POOL P

LOCATION (N.T.S)

CLARENDON POOL

ADDRESS: LIVERPOOL ST., SALFORD, M5 4AY
PHONE/FAX: 0161 736 1494 / 0161 737 0796
WEB/EMAIL: fit city clarendon@ sc.ll@co.uk
OWNER: SALFORD CITY COUNCIL

ELEVATION

MORRISSEY

SALFORD LADS CLUB

...GET SET...GO!

SALFORD'S GOT LOADS OF MUSICAL HEROES, AS WELL AS THE SUPERB QUAYS. OPENED IN 1984, THIS IMPRESSIVE LEISURE CENTRE PROUDLY BOASTS:

- MAIN POOL: 25M x 6 LANES
- TEACHING POOL (2 SHALLOW ENDS)
- HEALTH + FITNESS SUITE
- SPORTS HALL/AEROBIC STUDIO
- FREE PARKING ON SITE

JCM 19·10·10

ELITE LADY TRIATHLETES DIVING INTO SALFORD QUAYS

LOCATION (NTS)

N

SHOPS

POOL

P

THE CRESCENT

R

CROSS LANE

ALBION WAY

LIVERPOOL ST.

THE TING TINGS

ECCLES POOL

ADDRESS: BARTON LANE, ECCLES, SALFORD, M30 0DD
PHONE/FAX: 0161 787 7107/
WEB/EMAIL: fitcityeccles@scll.co.uk
OWNER: SALFORD CITY COUNCIL

ELEVATION

GEO. STEPHENSON'S "ROCKET" ~1830

YET ANOTHER GREAT POOL!
BIRTHPLACE OF ECCLES CAKES & ENGLAND
CRICKETER, MICHAEL VAUGHAN, ECCLES IS RIGHTLY
PROUD OF ITS ASSOCIATIONS WITH GEO. STEPHENSON'S
HISTORIC "MANCHESTER TO LIVERPOOL" RAILWAY.
OPENED IN 1988, THIS SUPERB COMPLEX OFFERS:

- POOL 25M × 5 LANES
- FITNESS SUITE + SPORTS HALL
- CAR PARKING (PAY + DISPLAY)

-DON'T FORGET TO SHOWER BEFORE SWIMMING!

GEORGE STEPHENSON

CHURCH ST.
R
IRWELL PL.
PP POOL
BARTON LANE
M
N
LOCATION (N.T.S)
JCM 0709-09

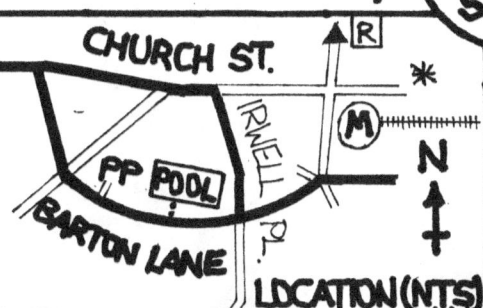

IRLAM + CADISHEAD LEISURE CENTRE

ADDRESS: LIVERPOOL RD., IRLAM, MCR., M44 6BR
PHONE/FAX: 0161 775 4134 / —
WEB/E-MAIL: fitcityirlam @ scll.co.uk
OWNER: SALFORD CITY COUNCIL

ELEVATION

JAMES WHITTAKER 36
SWAM ALL MILES OF THE SHIP CANAL ON 5+6 SEPT. 2008!

THIS IS A WORLD FIRST!

SITUATED ON THE NORTHERN BANK OF THE MANCHESTER SHIP CANAL, IRLAM BOASTS A SUPERB SWIMMING POOL - I AM REALLY IMPRESSED! OPENED IN 1966 AND EXTENSIVELY RENOVATED IN 2006, IT OFFERS:

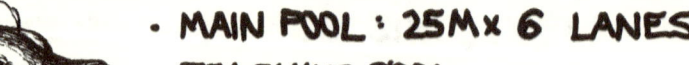

- MAIN POOL : 25M x 6 LANES
- TEACHING POOL
- HEALTH + FITNESS SUITE
- FREE CAR PARKING

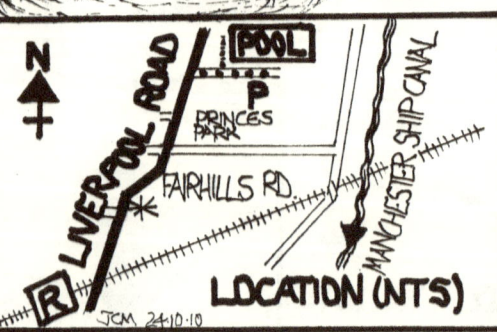

N

POOL
P
PRINCES PARK
LIVERPOOL ROAD
FAIRHILLS RD.
MANCHESTER SHIP CANAL
R
LOCATION (NTS)
JCM 24·10·10

30

PENDLEBURY POOL

ADDRESS: CROMWELL RD, PENDLEBURY, SALFORD, M27 9SZ
PHONE/FAX: 0161-793-1750/
WEB/E·MAIL: fitcitypendlebury@scll.co.uk
OWNER: SALFORD CITY COUNCIL

ELEVATION

- IMPROVE YOUR TECHNIQUE

ITS A JOY TO SWIM HERE! FOUNDED ON MINING AND RUGBY LEAGUE, THIS PLEASANT SUBURB HAS A SUPERB POOL. OPENED IN 1985, I FOUND STAFF + SWIMMERS VERY WELCOMING AND PROUD OF:

- POOL 25M x 6 LANES
- HEALTH + FITNESS SUITE
- SPORTS HALL
- FREE CAR PARKING

SPLASH

EXPERIENCED SWIMMERS WELCOME....

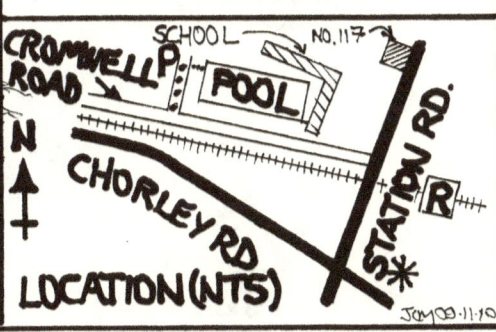

CROMWELL ROAD
SCHOOL
POOL
NO. 117
N
CHORLEY RD
STATION RD.
R
LOCATION (NTS)

JCM 00·11·10

L.S. LOWRY, ARTIST, LIVED AT 117 STATION RD.

31

WORSLEY POOL

ADDRESS: BRIDGEWATER ROAD, WALKDEN, WORSLEY, M28 3AB

PHONE/FAX: 0161 790 2084/

WEB/E-MAIL: fitcityworsley@scll.co.uk

OWNER: SALFORD CITY COUNCIL

ELEVATION

BRIDGE-WATER CANAL, WORSLEY VILLAGE

JCM 06·12·08

WHAT A TREMENDOUS POOL! OPENED IN 1974 AND EXTENSIVELY REFURBISHED IN 2007 AT A COST OF £4M, THIS FRIENDLY CENTRE PROVIDES THIS INTRIGUING AREA WITH:

- LARGE POOL 25M × 6 LANES
- SMALL POOL
- FITNESS SUITE/AEROBIC STUDIO
- PARKING ON SITE (FREE)

BE COURTEOUS TO POOL STAFF...

-COS LIFEGUARDS LOOK AFTER YOU!

N.B. THE POOL IS ACTUALLY LOCATED IN WALKDEN!

HIGH ST.

MANCHESTER RD

POOL

BRIDGEWATER ROAD

A575

N

R

LOCATION (NTS)

ASHTON LEISURE CENTRE

ADDRESS: OLD ROAD, ASHTON·IN·MAKERFIELD, WN4 9TP
PHONE/FAX: 01942 720826/
WEB/E-MAIL: ACTIVE LIFE @ WLCT. ORG
OWNER: WIGAN METROPOLITAN BOROUGH COUNCIL

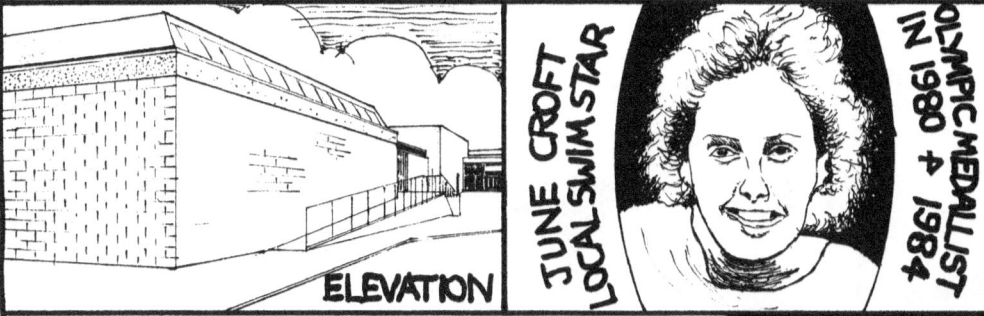

ELEVATION

JUNE CROFT LOCAL SWIM STAR

OLYMPIC MEDALLIST IN 1980 + 1984

WHAT A POPULAR POOL + FRIENDLY TOWN! OPENED IN 1977 + EXTENSIVELY REFURBISHED IN 2010, THIS LIVELY CENTRE OFFERS THE LOCAL COMMUNITY:

- LARGE POOL: 25m × 4 LANES
- SMALL POOL
- SPORTS HALL/FITNESS SUITE
- FREE CAR PARKING

COOL

L

ITS NEVER TOO LATE TO LEARN!

OLD RD.
WIGAN RD.
R
N
POOL
P
CANSFIELD GROVE
*
LOCATION (N.T.S)

WE PREFER IT SALTIER—

—COLDER—

—AND ALOT WETTER!

MEANWHILE, AT THE FISH MONGERS...

HINDLEY POOL

ADDRESS: BORSDANE AVENUE, HINDLEY, WIGAN, WN2 3QN
PHONE/FAX: 01942 255401 /
WEB/E-MAIL: ACTIVE LIFE @ WLCT.ORG
OWNER: WIGAN METROPOLITAN BOROUGH COUNCIL

ELEVATION

THEY SAY THAT ONCE A SWIMMER YOU ARE ALWAYS A SWIMMER....

THIS POOL PROVIDES A TREMENDOUS ASSET TO THE LOCAL COMMUNITY - YOU MUST SUPPORT IT! OPENED IN 1971, IT OFFERS:

- MAIN POOL: 25M × 6L
- SMALL POOL

JCM 06·02·12

REMEMBER TO SHOWER BEFORE

CONTACT HINDLEY LEISURE CENTRE ON 01942-253142 FOR DETAILS OF OTHER LOCAL FACILITIES.

-TURNED OUT NICE AGAIN!

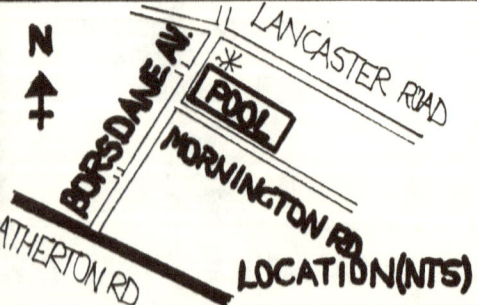

AND AFTER YOUR SWIM!

N

BORSDANE AV.
LANCASTER ROAD
POOL
MORNINGTON RD
ATHERTON RD.

LOCATION (NTS)

GEORGE FORMBY ENTERTAINER LIVED ON ATHERTON RD. AS A BOY

HOWE BRIDGE SPORTS CENTRE

ADDRESS: ECKERSLEY FOLD LANE, ATHERTON, MCR, M46 0PJ
PHONE/FAX: 01942 870403 / 01942 884376
WEB/E-MAIL: WWW.WLCT.ORG
OWNER: WIGAN METROPOLITAN BOROUGH COUNCIL

ELEVATION

HEATHER FREDERIKSEN, PARALYMPIC GOLD MEDALLIST 2008/2012 + LEIGH SWIMMER

DEEP END

OPENED IN 1977 AT A COST OF £1·3M, THIS FANTASTIC CENTRE IS A CREDIT TO THE COMMUNITY AND OFFERS SO MANY FACILITIES:
- MAIN POOL : 25M × 6 LANES
- TEACHING POOL
- HEALTH + FITNESS SUITE
- SPORTS HALL / COURTS
- FREE CAR PARKING

JEM 22·04·11

YOU WILL ENJOY YOUR SWIM!

- OR ELSE..

OLYMPIC GOLD MEDAL

ATHERLEIGH WAY
LOVERS LANE
LEIGH ROAD
ECKERSLEY FOLD LANE
POOL
P
N
ONE WAY SYSTEM

LOCATION (NTS)

LEIGH INDOOR SPORTS CENTRE

ADDRESS: SALE WAY, LEIGH, LANCS., WN7 4JY
PHONE/FAX: 01942 487800/01942 767514
WEB/E-MAIL: WWW.WLCT.ORG/ACTIVELIFE
OWNER: WIGAN METROPOLITAN BOROUGH COUNCIL

ELEVATION OF POOL

MAKE FRIENDS
WHEN YOU
SWIM!

THIS POOL IS SUPERB!
OPENED ON 02 JANUARY 2008, THIS £6.4M
CENTRE FORMS THE HEART OF THE AMBITIOUS
LEIGH SPORTS VILLAGE. FACILITIES ARE
SOME OF THE VERY BEST IN THE NORTH WEST:-
- MAIN POOL;
  25M × 6 LANES
- SPORTS HALL
- HEALTH AND
  FITNESS STUDIOS
- CAR PARKING-FREE

TWIST LANE
ATHERLEIGH WAY
SALE WAY
EAST LANCS RD.
P POOL
N
NO PATH FROM LEIGH
LOCATION (N.T.S.)

LEIGH
REMAINS
TRUE TO
RUGBY
LEAGUE

WIGAN LIFE CENTRE

ADDRESS: COLLEGE AVENUE, WIGAN, WN1 1NJ
PHONE/FAX: 01942 489611, 489612/
WEB/E-MAIL: WWW.WLCT.ORG/ACTIVELIFE
OWNER: WIGAN METROPOLITAN BOROUGH COUNCIL

ELEVATION

WIGAN WASPS SWIMMING CLUB HAS PRODUCED MANY CHAMPIONS SINCE 1896!

THIS CENTRE IS STUNNING! WIGAN NOW HAS A TOP CLASS VENUE TO COMPLEMENT ITS FAMOUS PIER, CHARACTERS, PIES AND OTHER SPORTING ASSOCIATIONS. OPENED IN 2011 AS PART OF A £67M REDEVELOPMENT OF COUNCIL FACILITIES, IT FEATURES:

- MAIN POOL - 25M × 8L WITH MOVEABLE FLOOR
- TEACHING POOL · SAUNA + STEAM SUITE
- HEALTH + FITNESS SUITE (GYM + STUDIOS)

STUART MACONIE BROADCASTER

GEORGE ORWELL WROTE "THE ROAD TO WIGAN PIER" IN 1937

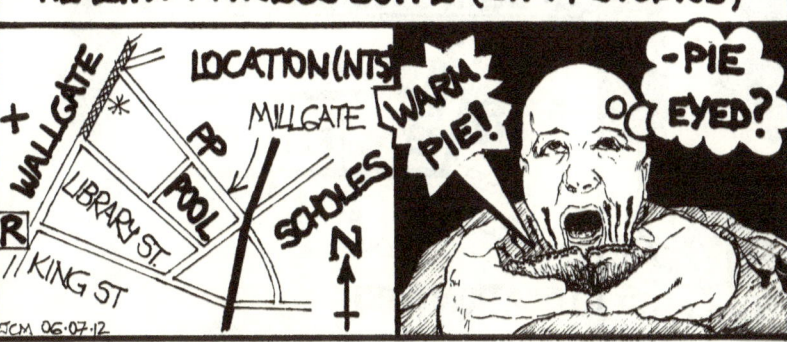

LOCATION (NTS)

WALLGATE · MILLGATE · LIBRARY ST. · PP POOL · SCHOLES · KING ST · N

WARM PIE!

-PIE EYED?

JCM 06·07·12

TYLDESLEY PELICAN CENTRE

ADDRESS: CASTLE ST., TYLDESLEY, M/C, M29 8EG
PHONE/FAX: 01942-882722/
WEB/E-MAIL: WWW.PELICANTYLDESLEY.CO.UK
MANAGED BY THE PELICAN CENTRE FROM 01-04-2012

ELEVATION

ASTLEY GREEN'S STEAM MUSEUM HAS THE ONLY SURVIVING PIT HEAD IN THE REGION

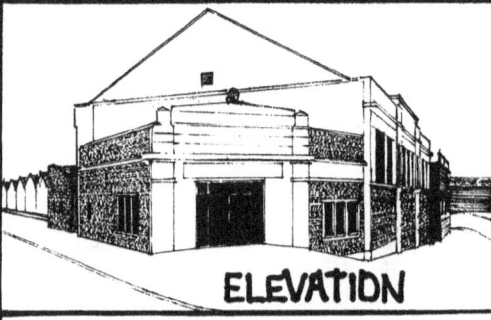

THIS FORMER PIT TOWN HAS NOT ONLY SUPPLIED 2 OLYMPIC + 1 PARALYMPIC SWIMMERS BUT ALSO FEATURES A POOL HOUSED IN A CONVERTED CINEMA! OPENED IN 1964 AT A COST OF £67,000, IT INCLUDES · MAIN POOL 25M x 5 LANES

THE OWD MINER

ADDIN TYLDESLEY

1908 100m OLYMPICS

TYLDESLEY SWIMMING + WATER POLO CLUB IS PROUD OF BEING FOUNDED IN 1876!

THE POOL'S DEEP; TRUST ME!

N

CASTLE ST
POOL

SHUTTLE ST.

ELLIOTT ST.

SQUIRES LANE

TOP CHAPEL

WARNING! NO POOL PARKING

LOCATION (NTS)

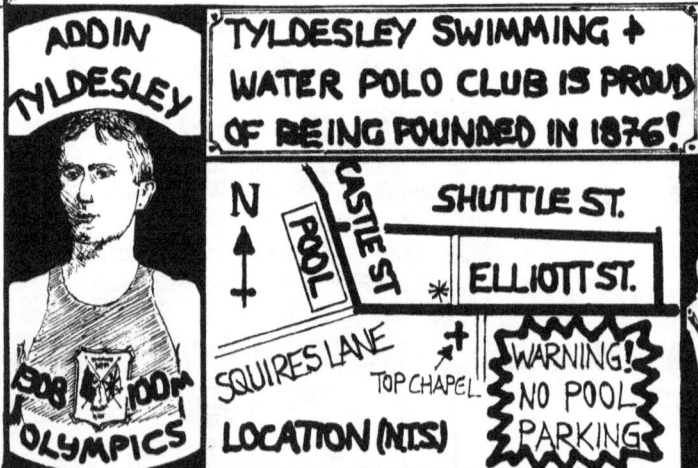

BOLTON ONE

ADDRESS: MOOR LANE, BOLTON, BL3 5BN
PHONE/FAX: 01204 374 910/
WEB/E-MAIL: WWW.BOLTONLEISURE.COM
OWNER: BOLTON METROPOLITAN BOROUGH COUNCIL

ELEVATION OF POOL

PETER KAY

FRED DIBNAH 1938 2004

STEEPLEJACK

THIS STUNNING CENTRE OF EXCELLENCE FOR HEALTH + WELL BEING WAS OPENED IN FEBRUARY 2012 AT A COST OF £31M. STATE OF THE ART FACILITIES INCLUDE:

- POOL 25M×8 LANES WITH MOVEABLE FLOOR
- THERAPEUTIC HYDROTHERAPY POOL
- FITNESS SUITE/COMMUNITY GYM
- DANCE + AEROBICS STUDIOS
- DISABLED CAR PARKING (CP)

GOING FOR GOLD!

JCM 100612
PP
MOOR LANE
B (BUS STATION)
TRINITY ST.
DEANE RD.
POOL
CP
UNIVERSITY
DERBY ST.
N
LOCATION (NTS)

THE FORMER BRIDGEMAN ST. BATHS WAS ONE OF THE FIRST PUBLIC BATHS TO OPEN IN THE UK: 1846 - 1976.

FARNWORTH LEISURE CENTRE

ADDRESS: BRACKLEY STREET, FARNWORTH,
BOLTON, LANCS, BL4 9DZ
PHONE/FAX: 01204 334477 /
WEB/E-MAIL: WWW.BOLTONLEISURE.COM
OWNER: BOLTON METROPOLITAN BOROUGH COUNCIL

POOL ELEVATION

THEY THINK THAT ITS ALL OVER ....IT IS NOW!

KENNETH WOLSTENHOLME, LOCAL COMMENTATOR

ITS A PLEASURE TO VISIT THIS DELIGHTFUL POOL + MEET SUCH FRIENDLY, HELPFUL STAFF. OPENED IN 1975, THE CENTRE PROVIDES THIS SMALL INDUSTRIAL TOWN WITH:

- MAIN POOL 25M × 6 LANES
- CHILDRENS POOL
- FITNESS ROOM
- PARKING ON SITE (FREE)

REMEMBER! YOUR POOL NEEDS

YOU!

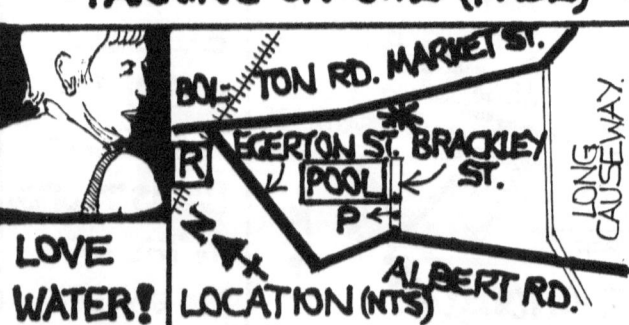

LOVE WATER!

LOCATION (NTS)

HORWICH LEISURE CENTRE

ADDRESS: VICTORIA ROAD, HORWICH,
BOLTON, BL6 5PY
PHONE/FAX: 01204 334488 / 01204 334434
WEB/E-MAIL: horwich.bolton@leisure.serco.com
OWNER: BOLTON METROPOLITAN BOROUGH COUNCIL

POOL ELEVATION

RIVINGTON PIKE FROM HORWICH

NO.1008; BUILT HORWICH 1889

JCM 230907

THE HISTORIC RAILWAY TOWN OF HORWICH, NESTLING BELOW RIVINGTON PIKE, IS A THRIVING COMMUNITY WITH MODERN FACILITIES eg REEBOK STADIUM. OPENED ON 29·03·1969, THE MAGNIFICENT POOL IS A CREDIT TO THIS PROUD + FRIENDLY TOWN AND OFFERS · LARGE   POOL 25M × 6 LANES
· SMALL POOL
· HEALTH SUITE

CHURCH ST/CHORLEY OLD RD.
PP
POOL
VICTORIA RD
PS
N
FS
CHORLEY NEW RD
LOCATION (NTS)

CRIKEY! THEY NEARLY SWIM AS WELL AS US!

41

SHARPLES COMMUNITY LEISURE CENTRE

ADDRESS: HILL COT ROAD, SHARPLES, BOLTON, BL1 8SN
PHONE/FAX: 0120 433 4224 /
WEB/E-MAIL: sharples.bolton@leisure.serco.com
OWNER: BOLTON METROPOLITAN BOROUGH COUNCIL

ELEVATION

TWO FAMOUS BOLTONIANS:

RADIO 1 DJ SARA J. COX

AND

BADLY DRAWN BOY

HELPFUL STAFF + FRIENDLY SWIMMERS HELPED MAKE MY FIRST VISIT TO THIS TINY OASIS VERY ENJOYABLE. AND ITS A RELAXING POOL, TO BOOT !
OPENED IN 1984, THIS CENTRE OFFERS:

- POOL 20M x 4 LANES
- GYM / SPORTS HALL
- FREE CAR PARKING

JFM 07·10·10

AAAARH! THE WATER'S FREEZING *

* IT SOON WARMS UP!

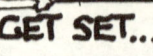

..GET SET...

MILL HILL COT RD.
BLACKBURN ROAD
P POOL
ASHWORTH LANE
N
* CROMPTON WAY
LOCATION (NTS)

SHOWER RAGE?

WESTHOUGHTON COMMUNITY L.C.

ADDRESS: BOLTON ROAD, WESTHOUGHTON,
BOLTON, LANCS., BL5 3BZ
PHONE/FAX: 01942 634810 /
WEB/E-MAIL: westhoughton.bolton@leisure.serco.com
OWNER: BOLTON METROPOLITAN BOROUGH COUNCIL

POOL ELEVATION

REEBOK STADIUM

BUILT IN ~1974, AND SITED ON THE TOWN'S
HIGH SCHOOL CAMPUS, THIS IMPRESSIVE BUT
COMPACT CENTRE PROVIDES THE "KEAW YEDS"
OF THIS FORMER PIT TOWN WITH:

JCM 24.11.08

- LARGE POOL 25M x 6 LANES
- SMALL POOL
- FITNESS SUITE
- PARKING ON SITE

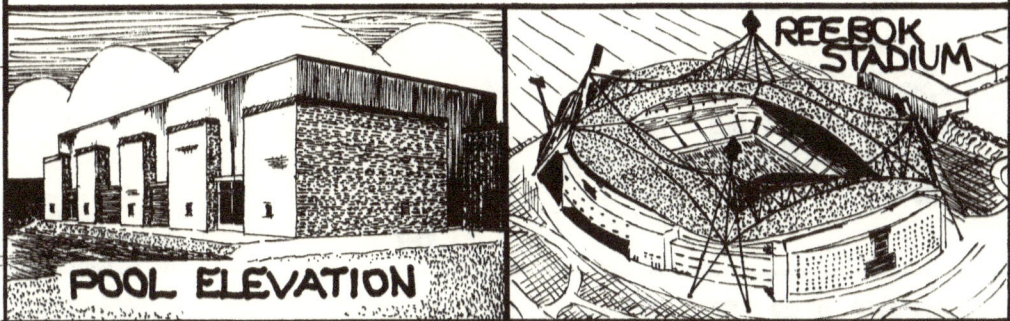

-B OF THE BANG!

PRETORIA
PIT TRAGEDY
MEMORIAL

DECEMBER 21ST
1910

PARK ROAD

POOL

P

MARKET ST.

BOLTON RD.

N

LOCATION (NTS)

CASTLE LEISURE CENTRE

ADDRESS: BOLTON ST., BURY, LANCS, BL9 0EZ
PHONE/FAX: 0161·253·7000 / -
WEB/E-MAIL: CASTLE. LEISURE @ BURY. GOV. UK
OWNER: BURY METROPOLITAN BOROUGH COUNCIL

POOL ELEVATION

LOCAL BAND ELBOW

BRIT AWARDS WINNER 2009!

FAMOUS FOR ITS BLACK PUDDINGS, OPEN MARKET,
EAST LANCASHIRE RAILWAY AND MILITARY HERITAGE,
BURY IS BOTH A BUSY AND POPULAR DESTINATION.
OPENED IN 1974, THIS IMPRESSIVE CENTRE OFFERS
A SUPRISING RANGE OF FACILITIES, INCLUDING :-
- MAIN POOL · 25M x 6 LANES
- TEACHING POOL
- DIVING POOL WITH { 1M SPRINGBOARD / 3M SPRINGBOARD / 5M PLATFORM
- BOOM POOL

WHY DON'T YOU LEARN TO DIVE?

LETS SWIM!

PEEL WAY   LOCATION (N.T.S)
JUBILEE WAY
BOLTON ST.
N
PP
POOL R MARKET ST.
IRWELL ST. PP
© JCM 22·04·10

RADCLIFFE POOL

ADDRESS: GREEN ST., RADCLIFFE, MANCHESTER, M26 3ED
PHONE/FAX: 0161 253 7000 /
WEB/E-MAIL: radcliffepool@bury.gov.uk
OWNER: BURY METROPOLITAN BOROUGH COUNCIL

ENTRANCE TO POOL

"THE METRO"

THE VISITOR TO THE SMALL TOWN OF RADCLIFFE MAY
WELL BE AMAZED BY THE SIZE ↑ PROPORTIONS
OF ITS SPACIOUS POOL. OPENED IN 1968, ITS DESIGN
SET A BENCHMARK FOR ANY NUMBER OF LOCAL
AUTHORITIES PLANNING TO BUILD POOLS IN THE 1970s.
IT FEATURES • MAIN POOL 25M x 6 LANES
           • SMALL POOL
           • GYM
           • PARKING ON SITE (FREE)

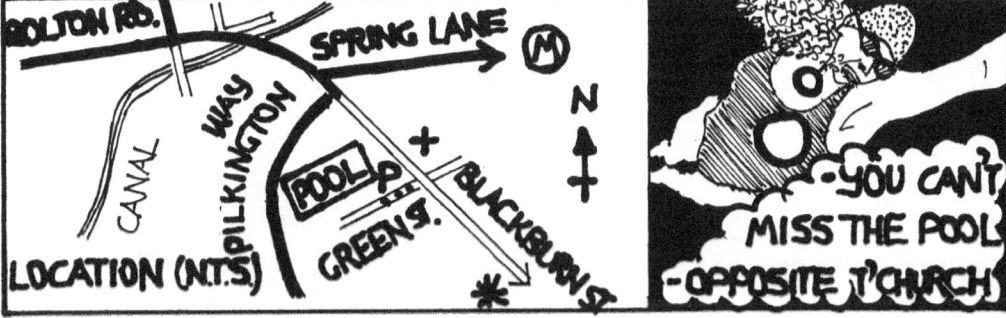

LOCATION (N.T.S)

- YOU CAN'T MISS THE POOL
- OPPOSITE T'CHURCH

RAMSBOTTOM POOL + FITNESS CENTRE

ADDRESS: PORRITT WAY, STUBBINS LANE,
RAMSBOTTOM, BURY, LANCS, BL0 0PT

PHONE/FAX: 0161 253 7000/

WEB/E-MAIL: ramsbottompool@bury.gov.uk

OWNER: BURY METROPOLITAN BOROUGH COUNCIL

M. PHELPS

ENTRANCE TO POOL

THIS POPULAR COMMUTER TOWN,
NESTLING BELOW HOLCOMBE HILL,
IS PROUD OF ITS COMPACT POOL.
PARTLY FUNDED BY BEQUEST FROM
THE LATE MISS PORRITT, THE POOL
FINALLY OPENED IN 1972 + FEATURES

- MAIN POOL 25M × 4 LANES
- GYM
- PARKING ON SITE (FREE)

PEEL TOWER
(128 FT. HIGH)

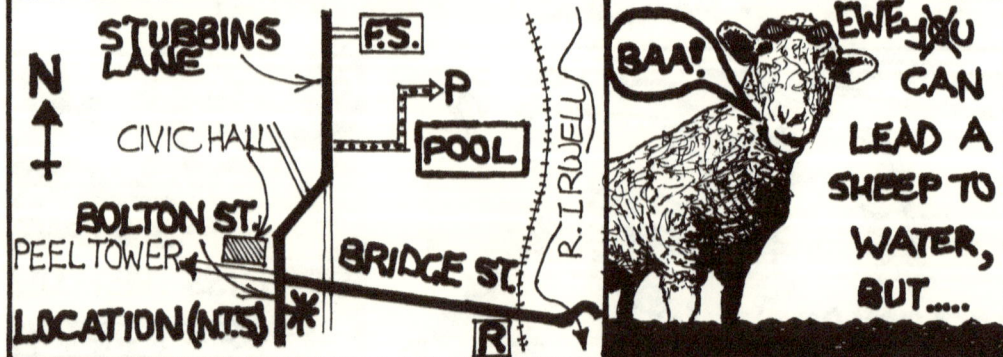

N

STUBBINS LANE
F.S.
P
POOL
CIVIC HALL
R. IRWELL
BOLTON ST.
PEEL TOWER
BRIDGE ST.
LOCATION (NTS)
R

BAA!

EWE YOU CAN LEAD A SHEEP TO WATER, BUT....

HEYWOOD SPORTS VILLAGE

ADDRESS: WEST STARKEY ST., HEYWOOD, LANCS, OL10 4TW
PHONE/FAX: 01706 924 000 / 0845 409 5082
WEB/E-MAIL: www.link4life.org/heywoodvillage
OWNER: ROCHDALE METROPOLITAN BOROUGH COUNCIL

ELEVATION OF POOL

WHY NOT GO BY EAST LANCS RAILWAY TO THE POOL?

WOW! WHAT A BRILLIANT FACILITY!!! OPENED IN OCTOBER 2010 BY HRH THE DUKE OF GLOUCESTER, THIS £10·4M INVESTMENT FEATURES:

- MAIN POOL: 25M × 6 LANES
- LEARNER POOL
- SPORTS HALL/OUTDOOR PITCHES
- EXERCISE AND FITNESS STUDIOS
- FREE CAR PARKING

HEYWOOD IS SO PROUD OF BOTH CHRISTINE GASKELL:
-COMMONWEALTH CHAMPION, 1974 AND KERI-ANNE PAYNE:
-WORLD CHAMPION, 2009.

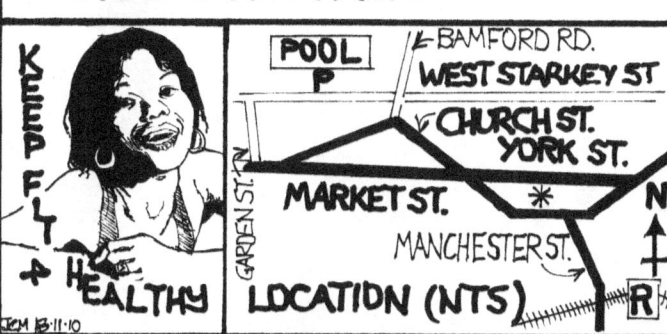

KEEP FIT & HEALTHY

POOL
P
BAMFORD RD.
WEST STARKEY ST
CHURCH ST.
YORK ST.
GARDEN ST.
MARKET ST.
MANCHESTER ST.
N
R
LOCATION (NTS)

JCM 13·11·10

MIDDLETON ARENA

ADDRESS: CORPORATION ST., MIDDLETON, M24 IAG
PHONE/FAX: 0161 682 4000/
WEB/E-MAIL: WWW.LINK4LIFE.ORG
OWNER: ROCHDALE METROPOLITAN BOROUGH COUNCIL

ELEVATION

KERI-ANNE PAYNE, OLYMPIC SILVER MEDALLIST, AT THE POOL OPENING

THE ARENA IS SUPERB! OPENED ON 4·1·2009, THIS IMPRESSIVE £15M SPORTS + ENTERTAINMENT CENTRE WILL HELP REGENERATE THE TOWN CENTRE + OFFER FIRST CLASS FACILITIES:

- MAIN POOL: 25M × 6 LANE
- TEACHING POOL
- SPORTS HALL + THEATRE
- FITNESS CENTRE / GYM
- PARKING ON SITE (FREE)

BOTH STEVE COOGAN, ACTOR + PAUL SCHOLES, FOOTBALLER, HAVE MIDDLETON ROOTS.

WILL THE REAL STEVE COOGAN STAND UP...?

LOCATION (NTS)
N
M62
MARKET PL.
ASSHETON WAY
HOLD HALL ST.
CORPORATION ST.
POOL
P
MIDDLETON SHOPPING CENTRE
*
B
M60
MIDDLETON WAY
A664
JCM 25·01·09

AHAH!

ROCHDALE LEISURE CENTRE

ADDRESS: ENTWISLE RD., ROCHDALE, OL16 2HZ
PHONE/FAX: 01706 926000
WEB/E-MAIL: WWW.LINK4LIFE.ORG
OWNER: ROCHDALE METROPOLITAN BOROUGH COUNCIL

ELEVATION

ROCHDALE PIONEERS: WORLD'S FIRST CO-OP IN c.1844

THIS ARCHETYPAL PENNINE MILLTOWN NOW HAS A £10·8M CENTRE TO IMPROVE PEOPLE'S HEALTH AND FITNESS! OPENED IN 2012, IT OFFERS:

- MAIN POOL - 25M x 8 LANES
- LEARNER POOL WITH MOVEABLE FLOOR
- SAUNA + STEAM ROOMS
- FITNESS SUITES/DANCE STUDIOS
- 4 COURT SPORTS HALL
- FREE CAR PARKING

JCM 180812

THIS TOWN ISN'T BIG ENUF FOR 2 POOLS!

ROCHDALE COWBOY

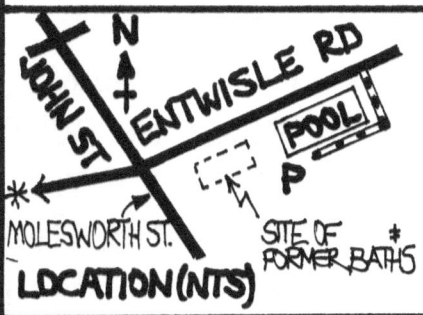

JOHN ST
N
ENTWISLE RD
POOL
P
MOLESWORTH ST.
SITE OF FORMER BATHS
LOCATION (NTS)

THE FORMER ART-DECO CENTRAL BATHS: 1937-2012

CHADDERTON WELLBEING CENTRE

ADDRESS: BURNLEY ST., CHADDERTON, OLDHAM, OL9 0JW
PHONE/FAX: 0161 770 5656/
WEB/E-MAIL: WWW.OCLACTIVE.CO.UK
OWNER: OLDHAM METROPOLITAN BOROUGH COUNCIL

ELEVATION

CHADDERTON'S HENRY TAYLOR AT THE 1908 LONDON OLYMPICS

THIS STRIKING CENTRE IS A UNIQUE STATE OF THE ART BUILDING HOSTING A RANGE OF MODERN FACILITIES. OPENED IN NOV 2009 AT A COST OF £9M, IT REPLACES THE FORMER ART DECO BATHS & FEATURES:

- HENRY TAYLOR POOL, 25M × 6 LANES
- FITNESS + AEROBIC DANCE STUDIOS
- LIBRARY/COMMUNITY ROOMS

JCM 01.06.11

SWIM TO WIN...

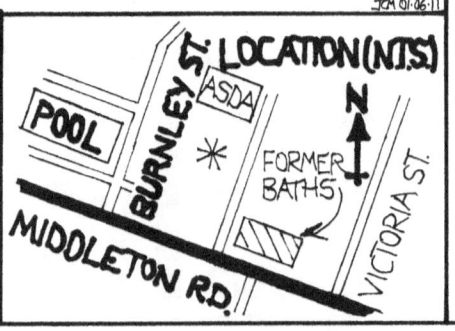

BURNLEY ST. LOCATION (N.T.S.)

POOL

ASDA

FORMER BATHS

MIDDLETON RD.

VICTORIA ST.

N

TAYLOR'S HAUL OF __3__ "GOLDS" AT LONDON HAS NEVER BEEN BETTERED! HE SWAM + INSTRUCTED AT THE FORMER BATHS FOR MUCH OF HIS LIFE.

CROMPTON POOL

ADDRESS: 5 FARROW ST., SHAW, OLDHAM, OL2 8NW
PHONE/FAX: 0161 207 7000/
WEB/E-MAIL: WWW.OCLACTIVE.CO.UK
OWNER: OLDHAM METROPOLITAN BOROUGH COUNCIL

ELEVATION

WINSTON CHURCHILL WAS ELECTED MEMBER OF PARLIAMENT FOR OLDHAM IN 1900

THIS IS A REAL TREASURE - OPENED IN 1899 AND NOW THE OLDEST POOL WITHIN GREATER MANCHESTER! THE HELPFUL STAFF ARE OBVIOUSLY VERY PROUD THAT ITS STILL OFFERS A GREAT SWIM.

FEATURES ARE:
- MAIN POOL 25yd x 10yd
- LEARNER POOL
- FITNESS SUITE

JRM 04-02-11

-DO YOU SWIM HERE OFTEN?

SWOON..

SHOBNA GULATI

LOCAL ACTOR

CROMPTON WAY
ROCHDALE RD. M
WESTWAY
FARROW ST.
LIBRARY
MARKET STREET
N
SHORT STAY CAR PARK
POOL
LOCATION (NTS)

ANOTHER ERA!

FAILSWORTH SPORTS CENTRE

ADDRESS: BRIERLEY AVENUE, FAILSWORTH, M35 9HA
PHONE/FAX: 061 207 7000/
WEB/E-MAIL: WWW.OCLACTIVE.CO.UK
OWNER: OLDHAM METROPOLITAN BOROUGH COUNCIL

ELEVATION

HENRY BRITAIN'S SWIMMING

TAYLOR, GREATEST CHAMPION: 1885-1951

I AM VERY IMPRESSED BY THIS PLEASANT POOL + FRIENDLY STAFF. OPENED IN 1982, THIS "GEM" OFFERS THE CLOSE-KNIT COMMUNITY:
- POOL: 25M x 4 LANES
- GYM AND FITNESS SUITE
- FREE PARKING ON SITE

T'POLE

JCM 26.07.09

BORN IN HOLLINWOOD, TAYLOR WON 3 GOLD MEDALS AT 1908 LONDON OLYMPICS!

NO LESS REMARKABLE IS DARA TORRES OF THE USA. SHE WON 3 SILVER MEDALS AT THE 2008 BEIJING OLYMPICS, AGED 41!

OLDHAM RD.
ASHTON
RD. EAST/WEB
BRIERLEY AVENUE
N
P POOL
SCHOOL
LOCATION (N.T.S.)

OLDHAM SPORTS CENTRE

ADDRESS: LORD STREET, OLDHAM, LANCS., OLI 3HA
PHONE/FAX: 0161 207 7000/0161 621 3224
WEB/E-MAIL: WWW.OCLACTIVE.CO.UK
OWNER: OLDHAM METROPOLITAN BOROUGH COUNCIL

ENTRANCE STEPS

ONCE WORLD FAMOUS FOR ITS COTTON MILLS, -AND HOME TO FISH₊CHIPS- OLDHAM IS PROUD OF ITS DIVERSE COMMUNITIES, SPORT, THEATRE & ARTS.

OPENED BY THE LATE RIGHT HONOURABLE DENIS HOWELL, MP ON 9 MAY 1975, THIS HIGHLY RECOMMENDED CENTRE FEATURES

- MAIN POOL - 33⅓m × 6 LANES
- DIVING POOL
- LEARNER POOL
- HEALTH SUITE & GYM

HOW HYGENIC TO INSTALL—

-PRE POOL SHOWERS

-THAT EVERY ONE HAS TO USE!

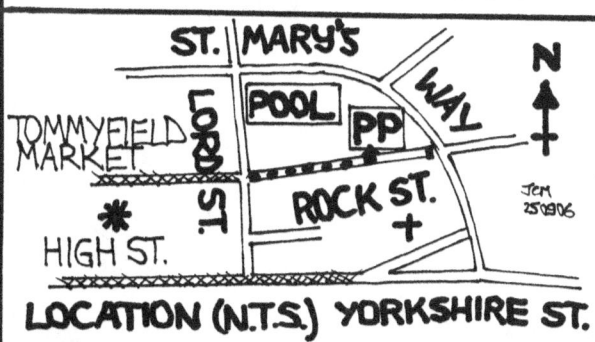

TOMMYFIELD MARKET
ST. MARY'S
LORD ST.
POOL
PP
WAY
N
HIGH ST.
ROCK ST.
JCM 25:09:06

LOCATION (N.T.S.) YORKSHIRE ST.

IF ONLY EVERY POOL WOULD FOLLOW SUITE!

ROYTON SPORTS CENTRE

ADDRESS: PARK ST., ROYTON, OLDHAM, OL2 6QW
PHONE/FAX: 0161 207-7000/
WEB/E-MAIL: WWW.OCLACTIVE.CO.UK
OWNER: OLDHAM METROPOLITAN BOROUGH COUNCIL

ELEVATION OF POOL

TWO LOCAL STARS IN FOR TEAM GB J.O'REGAN AND ELLA CHADDERTON

WATER POLO TRAINING SQUAD:

THIS FORMER MILL TOWN BOASTS MANY STUNNING EDWARDIAN BUILDINGS, AS WELL AS THE PUBLIC BATHS, OPENED IN 1910 AT A COST OF £8K + REFURBISHED IN 1962, IT'S SPAWNED SOME GREAT WATER POLO TEAMS.

HAVEN'T STYLES CHANGED!

FACILITIES OFFER:
- POOL - 25yd × 10yd
- FITNESS SUITE
- CRECHE

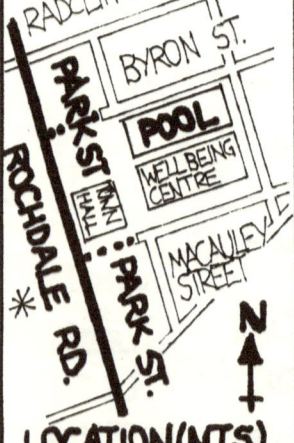

RADCLIFFE ST.
BYRON ST.
PARK ST.
POOL
WELLBEING CENTRE
TOWN HALL
ROCHDALE RD.
PARK ST.
MACAULEY STREET
*
N
LOCATION (NTS)

COTTON MILL LANDSCAPE

LIDO

SADDLEWORTH POOL & LEISURE CENTRE

ADDRESS: STATION ROAD, UPPERMILL,
OLDHAM, LANCS, OL3 6HQ
PHONE/FAX: 0161 207 7000/
WEB/E-MAIL: WWW.OCLACTIVE.CO.UK
OWNER: OLDHAM METROPOLITAN BOROUGH COUNCIL

ELEVATION

AMMON WRIGLEY, LOCAL POET

UPPERMILL VIADUCT

REMOTE SADDLEWORTH OOZES MOORLAND GRIT & ARTISTIC HERITAGE. OPENED IN 1973 ~ AND EXTENDED IN 2009 ~ THIS LOVELY FACILITY OFFERS:

- MAIN POOL - 25M × 4 LANES
- FITNESS SUITE & DANCE STUDIO
- SYNTHETIC PITCHES (OUTDOOR)
- FREE CAR PARKING

JCM 15.06.11

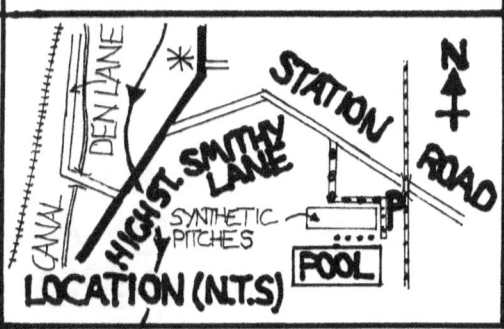

LOCATION (N.T.S)

T'ANNUAL BAND CONCERT CREATES WATER MUSIC!

ASHTON POOLS

ADDRESS: WATER STREET, ASHTON-UNDER-LYNE,
TAMESIDE, OL6 7AN

PHONE/FAX: 0161 330 1179 / 0161 343 3122

WEB/E-MAIL: WWW.TAMESIDESPORTSTRUST.COM

OWNER: TAMESIDE M.B.C.

ENTRANCE TO POOL   PORTLAND BASIN

EXTENSIVELY REFURBISHED IN 2005, THIS
PLEASANT AND DECEPTIVELY, SPACIOUS
TOWN CENTRE POOL WAS OPENED BY THE
LATE RIGHT HONOURABLE DENIS
HOWELL M.P., ON 30 APRIL 1975. IT
FEATURES • MAIN POOL 25 M x 6 LANES
• TEACHING POOL
• HEALTH SUITE AND GYM

JCM 13·09·12

LOCATION (N.T.S.)

-WHEN PARKING, SONNY, ALWAYS: PAY AND DISPLAY!

THE COPLEY CENTRE

ADDRESS: HUDDERSFIELD ROAD, STALYBRIDGE,
TAMESIDE, SK15 3ET
PHONE/FAX: 0161 303 8118 / 0161 303 8253
WEB/E-MAIL: WWW.TAMESIDESPORTSTRUST.COM
OWNER: TAMESIDE M.B.C.

ENTRANCE TO POOL

IT'S A LONG WAY TO TIPPERARY
JACK JUDGE, LOCAL COMPOSER

THIS DELIGHTFUL POOL OPENED IN APRIL 1979
AND OCCUPIES A LOVELY PENNINE SETTING
HIGH ABOVE STALYBRIDGE, A HISTORIC CANAL
TOWN WITH A BURGEONING "NIGHT SCENE."
IT OFFERS • SWIMMING POOL 25M × 6 LANES
• TEACHING POOL
• GYMNASIUM + WEIGHT TRAINING ROOM
• PARKING ON SITE (FREE)

JCM 240609

WAKEFIELD RD.
STAMFORD ST.
HUDDERSFIELD RD.
TO POOL
R
RIVER TAME
R. TAME CANAL
CANAL
MOTTRAM RD.
N
LOCATION (NTS)

AND WARM
DO COME ON IN - THE WATER'S LOVELY!

DENTON POOLS

ADDRESS: VICTORIA STREET, DENTON,
TAMESIDE, M34 9GU
PHONE/FAX: 0161 336 1900 / 0161 336 9156
WEB/EMAIL: WWW.TAMESIDESPORTSTRUST.COM
OWNER: TAMESIDE METROPOLITAN BOROUGH COUNCIL

ELEVATION

RICKY "HITMAN" HATTON LAS VEGAS JUNE 2007

STAR BILLING!

DENTON IS BLESSED WITH NEW DEVELOPMENTS + RICKY HATTON'S GYM. OPENED IN 1975 BY ANITA LONSBROUGH MBE, THIS POPULAR FACILITY PROVIDES:
- MAIN POOL 25M × 6 LANES
- SMALL POOL + SUNBED UNIT
- PARKING ON SITE (FREE)

JCM 03·12·08

LOCATION (NTS)

CROWN POINT

N M67
MANCHESTER RD. HYDE RD

VICTORIA ST. P POOL

STOCKPORT ROAD

SWIMMING: ONE OF LIFE'S (SIMPLE) PLEASURES...

DUKINFIELD POOL

ADDRESS: BIRCH LANE, DUKINFIELD, TAMESIDE, SK16 5AP
PHONE/FAX: 0161 330 5208/0161 308 4394
WEB/E-MAIL: WWW.TAMESIDESPORTSTRUST.COM
OWNER: TAMESIDE METROPOLITAN BOROUGH COUNCIL

POOL ELEVATION

WILL THE 'REAL' COLONEL ROBERT DUKINFIELD. (CIVIL WAR HERO)·PLEASE STAND UP?

THIS CLOSE KNIT HISTORICAL MILL TOWN CAN BOAST CIVIL WAR TIES AND TV's "NORA BATTY'S" BIRTH PLACE (THE LATE KATHY STAFF). OPENED IN 1965, THIS SPACIOUS POOL OFFERS AN ENJOYABLE SWIM WITH

- POOL 25M x 6 LANES
- HEALTH SUITE/SUN BEDS
- FREE CAR PARKING

JCM 18·05·10

-CALL THAT SWIMMING?

GO ON....SWIM FOR IT!

-HA,HA!

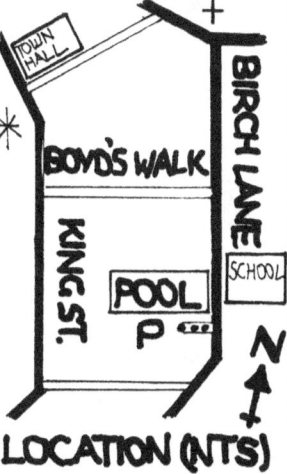

TOWN HALL

BOYD'S WALK

KING ST.

BIRCH LANE

SCHOOL

POOL P

N

LOCATION (NTS)

MEDLOCK LEISURE CENTRE

ADDRESS: GARDEN FOLD WAY, OFF MARKET ST.,
DROYLSDEN, M43 7XU
PHONE/FAX: 0161 370 3070/0161 301 4377
WEB/E-MAIL: WWW.TAMESIDESPORTSTRUST.COM
OWNER: TAMESIDE M.B.C.

POOL ENTRANCE

MOSCOW OLYMPIC SILVER MEDALLIST, POPULAR BROADCASTER + CELEBRITY. SHARRON DAVIES

OPENED BY SHARRON DAVIES IN JANUARY 2006,
+ BUILT FOR £4m, THIS SPACIOUS POOL HELPS
"PROVIDE FACILITIES AS GOOD AS YOU'D FIND IN
THE PRIVATE SECTOR." (COUNCIL LEADER).
IT OFFERS • SWIMMING POOL 25M × 6 LANES
• FITNESS SUITE + DANCE STUDIO
• PARKING ON SITE (FREE)

JCM 29.12.10

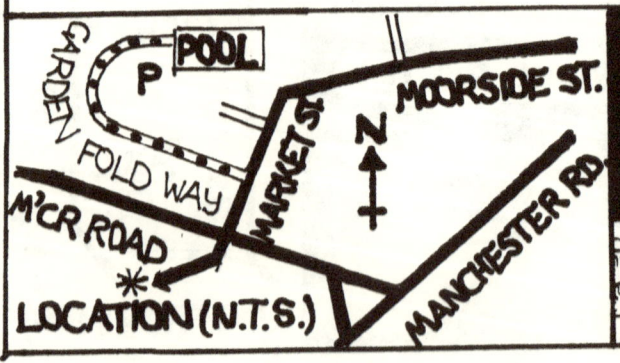
GARDEN FOLD WAY
POOL
P
MARKET ST.
N
MOORSIDE ST.
MANCHESTER RD.
M'CR ROAD
LOCATION (N.T.S.)

UM...YET MORE WATER!

AVONDALE

ADDRESS: HEATHBANK RD., CHEADLE HEATH, SK3 0UP
PHONE/FAX: 0161 - 477 - 4242 /
WEB/E-MAIL: WWW.LIFELEISURE.NET
OWNER: STOCKPORT METROPOLITAN BOROUGH COUNCIL

ELEVATION

SWIMMING IS BRILLIAAANT!

LOCALS HAVE CAMPAIGNED SUCCESSFULLY TO SAVE THIS POPULAR FACILITY. LOCATED IN THE GROUNDS OF STOCKPORT ACADEMY, IT PROVIDES:
- POOL 25M × 5 LANES
- FITNESS SUITE/GYM
- SPORTS HALL
- FREE CAR PARKING

JCM 24-11-11

WHY NOT LEARN TO DIVE?

AS CHEAP AS CHIPS!

DAVID DICKINSON WAS BORN IN CHEADLE HEATH

P
POOL P
STOCKPORT ACADEMY
HEATHBANK RD.
BIRD HALL LANE
EDGELEY RD.
N
LOCATION (NTS)

CHEADLE

ADDRESS: SHIERS DRIVE, CHEADLE, STOCKPORT, SK8 1JR
PHONE/FAX: 0161 428 3216
WEB/E·MAIL: WWW.LIFELEISURE.NET
OWNER: STOCKPORT METROPOLITAN BOROUGH COUNCIL

ELEVATION

SWIMMING IS PURE "ME TIME"!

CHEADLE IS AN UPMARKET, SOPHISTICATED VILLAGE WITH AN EXCEPTIONAL SPORTS CENTRE. LOCATED IN A DELIGHTFUL PARKLAND, OPENED IN 1974, IT OFFERS:

- MAIN POOL 33⅓M × 6L
- SMALL POOL
- FITNESS SUITE
- AEROBICS STUDIO
- FREE CAR PARKING

IT'S <u>JUST</u> NOT FAIR! SOME PEOPLE GET ALL THE VERY BEST POOLS!

ANGLIAN CROSS CIRCA 11ᵗʰ CENTURY FOUND NEAR THE PARISH CHURCH. CHANGED IN 1975.

CHEADLE CROSS - 11ᵗʰ CENTURY

LOCATION (NTS) SHIERS DRIVE

N

POOL
P
P

HIGH ST.

WILMSLOW RD

BROADWAY

JCM 070412

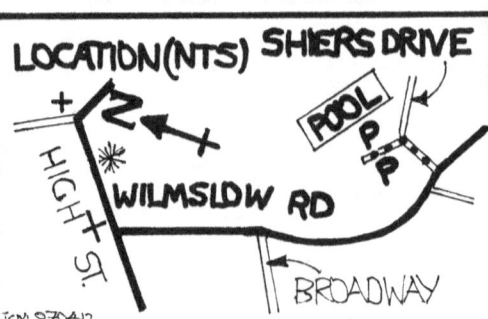

GRAND CENTRAL POOLS

ADDRESS: 2 GRAND CENTRAL SQUARE,
WELLINGTON RD. SOUTH, STOCKPORT,
CHESHIRE, SK1 3TA

PHONE/FAX: 0161 474 7766/

WEB/E-MAIL: WWW.LIFELEISURE.NET

OWNER: STOCKPORT METROPOLITAN BORO COUNCIL

ELEVATION FROM RAILWAY ROAD

STOCKPORT MARKET FROM ST. MARY'S CHURCH

GRAND BY NAME + GRAND BY NATURE...
STOCKPORT CAN BE JUSTIFIABLY PROUD
OF BOTH ITS OLYMPIC SIZED SWIMMING
POOL AND THE CONTINUING SUCCESSES
OF STOCKPORT METRO SWIMMING CLUB
WHICH TRAINS THERE. SEE WHAT I MEAN:-

CASSIE PATTEN

· OLYMPICS ·	WORLD CHAMP'S.
GRAEME SMITH - BRONZE 1996 ATLANTA	GRAEME SMITH - SILVER 2001 JAPAN
STEVE PARRY - BRONZE 2004 ATHENS	CASSIE PATTEN - SILVER 2007 MELBOURNE + 2008 SELVILLE
KERI-ANNE PAYNE - SILVER CASSIE PATTEN - BRONZE 2008 BEIJING	KERI-ANNE PAYNE - GOLD 2009 ROME + 2011 SHANGHAI

JCM 070508

GRAND CENTRAL POOLS

BRANDED "THE JEWEL IN STOCKPORT'S LEISURE CROWN", THE POOLS OPENED IN APRIL 1993 AT A COST OF £9 MILLION + FEATURE:
- MAIN POOL 50m × 8 LANES WITH "FLOATING" FLOOR
- LEISURE LAGOON
- GYM / HEALTH SUITE

DESPITE INITIAL CONCERNS OVER POOL FUNDING, THE POOLS WERE BUILT TO TIME AND BUDGET.

RENOWNED AS A TEXTILE PRODUCER OF SILK + HATS, STOCKPORT'S "CREDIBILITY" IMPROVED IN THE 1970's

JFM 290907

+ 80's WHEN "STRAWBERRY STUDIOS" RECORDED SUPERBANDS LIKE "10 CC", "THE SMITHS" + "NEW ORDER"

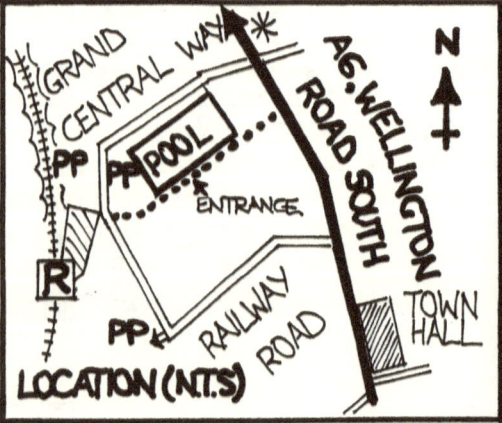

GRAND CENTRAL WAY
A6. WELLINGTON ROAD SOUTH
N
PP
POOL
ENTRANCE
PP
R
PP
RAILWAY ROAD
TOWN HALL
LOCATION (N.T.S)

ALL THIS + WATER POLO, AS WELL!

HAZEL GROVE

ADDRESS: JACKSON'S LANE, HAZEL GROVE, SK7 5JW
PHONE/FAX: 0161 439 5221 /
WEB/E-MAIL: WWW.LIFELEISURE.NET
OWNER: STOCKPORT METROPOLITAN BOROUGH COUNCIL

ELEVATION OF POOL

HAZL GROVE'S PROSPERITY HAS BENEFITTED FROM ITS PROXIMY TO THE BUSY A6 MAIN ROAD. OPENED IN 1974, THIS IMPRESSIVE CENTRE OFFERS A MEMORABLE SWIM AND FEATURES:

- MAIN POOL, 25M X 6 LANES
- FITNESS SUITE
- AEROBIC STUDIO
- SPIN STUDIO
- FREE CAR PARKING
- SMALL POOL
- CRECHE

-LOVE WATER, LOVE SWIMMING!

DEEP END

LOCATION (NTS)

BRAMHALL MOOR LANE
BUXTON RD, A6
P POOL
MACCLESFIELD ROAD
R
JACKSON'S LANE
N

MARPLE LEISURE CENTRE

ADDRESS: STOCKPORT ROAD, MARPLE, SK6 6AA
PHONE/FAX: 0161·427·7070/
WEB/E-MAIL: WWW. LIFELEISURE. NET
OWNER: STOCKPORT METROPOLITAN BOROUGH COUNCIL

ELEVATION

MATTHEW WALKER, MBE: LOCAL SWIMMER AND CHAMPION PARALYMPIC

THIS IS A LOVELY, LITTLE POOL AND WELL WORTH VISITING! STAFF ARE OBLIGING + SWIMMERS FRIENDLY. OPENED IN 1931, THIS TRADITIONAL FACILITY PROVIDES LOCAL RESIDENTS WITH A POPULAR HAVEN OFFERING:

- MAIN POOL - 25 YDS × 4 LANES
- FITNESS SUITE
- CAR PARKING - PAY + DISPLAY

MARPLE SITS AT THE JUNCTION OF PEAK FOREST + MACCLESFIELD CANALS.

LOCATION (N.T.S)

THE BATHS WERE PRESENTED TO THE PEOPLE OF MARPLE IN LOVING MEMORY OF ANDREW MACNAIR

66

ROMILEY

ADDRESS: HOLEHOUSE FOLD, ROMILEY, SK6 4BB
PHONE/FAX: 0161·430·3437/
WEB/E-MAIL: WWW. LIFELEISURE.NET
OWNER: STOCKPORT METROPOLITAN BOROUGH COUNCIL

ELEVATION

WARNING!
- SWIMMING EXERCISES THOSE PARTS THAT OTHER SPORTS DON'T EVEN KNOW EXIST!

SITUATED "ONLY 5 MINUTES" FROM THE CENTRE OF UPMARKET ROMILEY, THIS FINE CENTRE GIVES THE LOCAL COMMUNITY:
- MAIN POOL 25M × 5L
- SMALL POOL
- FITNESS SUITE
- AEROBICS STUDIO
- SAUNA/STEAM+THERAPY ROOMS
- FREE CAR PARKING

JCM 13.04.12

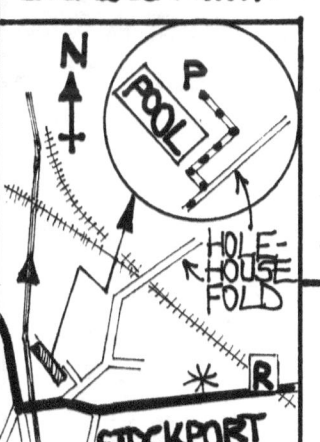

LOCATION (N.T.S.)

TONY O'SHEA
LOCAL HERO
DARTS SUPREMO

THE POOL WAS OPENED ON 7 JULY 1973 BY DIANA WILKINSON. STOCKPORT BORN, SHE SWAM IN BOTH THE 1960 + 1964 OLYMPICS.

COLLIER STREET BATHS
(HISTORIC POOL)

ADDRESS: COLLIER ST., GREENGATE, SALFORD, M3 7DW

DISTRICT: SALFORD CITY COUNCIL (GRADE 2*)

FAMOUS RIVER IRWELL LIFESAVER + SWIMMING TEACHER AT BATHS

MARK ADDY 1838 1890 "SALFORD HERO"

THIS IS BRITAIN'S OLDEST SURVIVING SWIMMING BATHS BUILDING! OPENED IN 1856 AT A COST OF £9,931, IT WAS THE MANCHESTER + SALFORD BATHS + LAUNDRIES CO'S FIRST POOL. IT CLOSED IN 1880 AND NOW LIES DERELICT. ORIGINAL FACILITIES WERE:

- FIRST CLASS BATHS · 53' x 25'
- SECOND CLASS BATHS · 53' x 25'
- VAPOUR AND SLIPPER BATHS

THE MANCHESTER + SALFORD BATHS + LAUNDRIES COMPANY WAS SET UP IN 1855 - AND BUILT A TOTAL OF 5 PUBLIC BATHS. THE COMPANY WAS ACQUIRED IN 1875 BY MANCHESTER CORP^{ON}

T. WORTHINGTON ARCHITECT OF BATHS

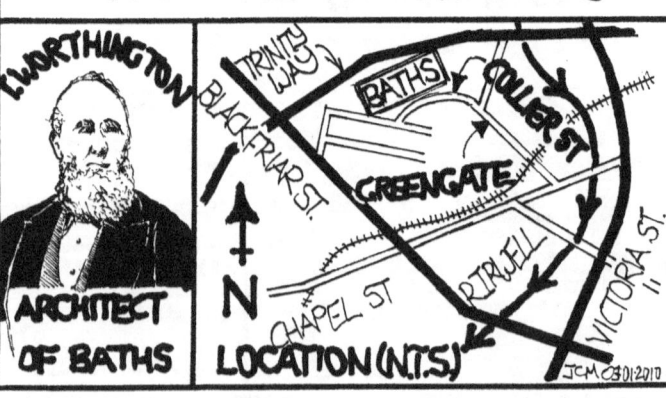

LOCATION (N.T.S.)

TRINITY WAY · BLACKFRIAR ST. · BATHS · COLLIER ST · GREENGATE · CHAPEL ST · R. IRWELL · VICTORIA ST. · N · JCM 03·01·2010

MANCHESTER AND SALFORD BATHS + LAUNDRIES CORPORATION ANNO DOMINI MDCCCLV

BATHS PLAQUE

VICTORIA BATHS
(HISTORIC POOL)

ADDRESS: HATHERSAGE ROAD, CHORLTON-ON-
           MEDLOCK, MANCHESTER, M13 OFE

PHONE/FAX: 0161-224-2020/

WEB/E-MAIL: WWW.VICTORIABATHS.ORG.UK

OWNER: MANCHESTER CITY COUNCIL

THE "WATER PALACE"

HOW DARE ANYONE FORGET THE VICTORIA BATHS!

DESCRIBED AS "THE MOST SPLENDID MUNICIPAL BATHING INSTITUTION IN THE COUNTRY", THESE ORNATE EDWARDIAN BATHS WERE OPENED ON 7 SEPTEMBER 1906 AT A (THEN) STAGGERING COST OF £59 000! SADLY, THEY CLOSED IN 1993.

LOCAL SWIMMER, SUNNY → LOWRY, SWAM THE CHANNEL IN 1933.

MALES 1ST CLASS/GALA POOL

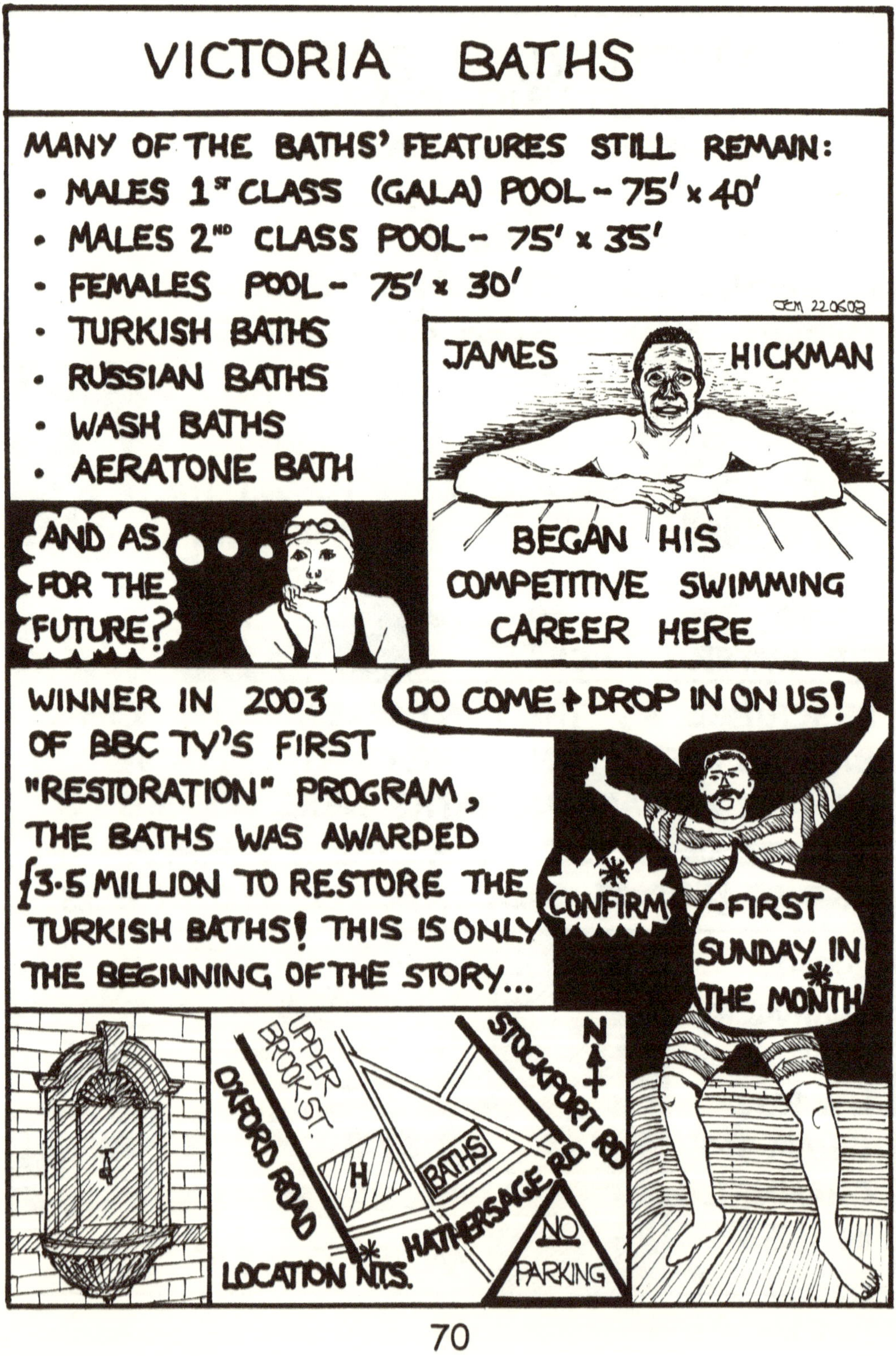

VICTORIA BATHS

MANY OF THE BATHS' FEATURES STILL REMAIN:
- MALES 1st CLASS (GALA) POOL — 75' x 40'
- MALES 2nd CLASS POOL — 75' x 35'
- FEMALES POOL — 75' x 30'
- TURKISH BATHS
- RUSSIAN BATHS
- WASH BATHS
- AERATONE BATH

JCM 220608

JAMES HICKMAN BEGAN HIS COMPETITIVE SWIMMING CAREER HERE

AND AS FOR THE FUTURE?

WINNER IN 2003 OF BBC TV'S FIRST "RESTORATION" PROGRAM, THE BATHS WAS AWARDED {3.5 MILLION TO RESTORE THE TURKISH BATHS! THIS IS ONLY THE BEGINNING OF THE STORY...

DO COME + DROP IN ON US!

CONFIRM

—FIRST SUNDAY IN THE MONTH

UPPER BROOK ST.
OXFORD ROAD
STOCKPORT RD.
N
BATHS
H
HATHERSAGE RD.
NO PARKING
LOCATION NTS.

INDEX OF POOLS

INDEX OF POOLS